The essence of wisdom is taking what is complicated and not making it simple, but offering a clarity that cuts to the chase of a matter. Rod Wilson is a wise, compelling, and true-to-the-heart human whose gift of clarity is scintillating and life-changing. To take three common but often misused phrases and offer a robust picture of what they can bring to life is brilliant, but far more, it is a reminder of how our words reflect the genius of our Creator. This book will bring a new savor to the sweetness and saltiness of your words.

DAN B. ALLENDER, PHD, professor of counseling psychology and founding president, The Seattle School of Theology and Psychology

Are we happy about the way we respond to and interact with the people in our lives? If we know we are falling short, failing to treat with respect and understanding the precious people whose lives are linked with ours, three phrases excavated and explicated by Rod Wilson may go a long way to enhance mutual harmony and trust. I know these are principles I need to learn and practice!

LUCI SHAW, author of *Angels Everywhere* and *The Thumbprint in the Clay*, writer in residence at Regent College

Sometimes we have to talk ourselves into becoming different people. We believe what we repeat. We live into what we rehearse. In this wise and inviting book, Rod Wilson offers us three simple but potent lit........ could talk us into becoming a socie........

caring, vulnerable, and grateful. Don't let what seems like simplicity fool you: This is a book that wants to change the world. It starts with me. And you.

JAMES K. A. SMITH, professor of philosophy at Calvin University, author of *You Are What You Love*

Rod is like a good spiritual-retreat master, only more humorous. After reading Rod Wilson, I'll never again trivialize the importance of saying "Thank you," "I'm sorry," and "Tell me more." These expressions pack a wallop and, when understood, found a needed culture based on gratitude, remorse, and caring.

J. MICHAEL MILLER, CSB, archbishop of Vancouver

It is amazing that so much is packed into three magical phrases totaling seven words! I am awed by Rod's ability to unpack them with the aid of engaging, first-person stories. The nuances revealed are rich in spiritual and psychological implications. They are so profoundly applicable in changing my own mindset that I could not read through it without constantly stopping to apply the principles to my own life.

WILLIAM WAN, JP, PHD, general secretary, Singapore Kindness Movement

With his poignant, insightful, and often witty slices of real-life wisdom, Dr. Wilson shines a light on ways we might embrace the much-needed practices of gratitude, remorse, and care to bring connection and gracious humility to an increasingly fractured and self-centered world. If we allow this thoughtful book to challenge us to use the three key phrases of "Thank you," "I'm sorry," and "Tell me more" meaningfully in everyday life, we might slow down enough to relate to one another in healing and affirming ways.

KEREN DIBBENS-WYATT, Christian contemplative, author of *Recital of Love*

This is the best time in human history to be alive. And yet so many of us are unthankful. Rod Wilson's stories of gratitude, remorse, and caring open us up to seeing how we've been captivated by entitlement, victimization, and individualism. Those stories can also help us laugh at ourselves and enjoy the journey to our better selves.

BOB INGLIS, US representative (R-SC4) 1993–1999, 2005– 2011; executive director of republicEn, South Carolina

Timely in an age of division and polarization. Laced with tender stories from his own life. Rod applies three familiar yet revolutionary simple statements that can transform relationships, organizations, cities, and our world. Honest, heart-warming, vulnerable, and at times raw, Rod lives what he writes.

REV. DR. MICHELE A. BLAND, senior pastor and psychologist, Hong Kong

This book came into my life at the exact right time. As I have faced being a CEO, wife, and mother of six in a world that seems to be filled with increasing discontent, discord, and disconnection, Dr. Wilson so clearly articulates how three simple phrases can help me bring more love, hope, and connection into my personal and professional lives. Dr. Wilson's expert storytelling reveals how gratitude, remorse, and caring enough to listen to others' stories can transform the world. This is THE must-read book for anyone who is leading through challenge and uncertainty.

ALIA EYRES, CEO of Mother's Choice, Hong Kong

In an age when there is an oversupply of self-proclaimed leaders and an undersupply of humility, Rod Wilson is a skillful leader with a humble and caring heart. In his latest book, he taps into the universal values of gratitude, contrition, and curiosity as key tools in a leader's toolbox. This is timeless wisdom, and I have had the pleasure of seeing Rod live these values in real life. He walks the walk.

PATRICIA TOWLER, president and CEO of CPA Nova Scotia, Canada

Thank You. I'm Sorry. Tell Me More.

Thank You.

How to Change the World

I'm Sorry.

with 3 Sacred Sayings

Tell Me More.

Rod Wilson

*A NavPress resource published in alliance
with Tyndale House Publishers*

NavPress

NavPress is the publishing ministry of The Navigators, an international Christian organization and leader in personal spiritual development. NavPress is committed to helping people grow spiritually and enjoy lives of meaning and hope through personal and group resources that are biblically rooted, culturally relevant, and highly practical.

For more information, visit NavPress.com.

This book is dedicated to a much-loved group of people:

my daughter, Jessica Noel,

my nieces and nephews, and their spouses: Lindsey, Luke, Madeleine, Nate, Jenna, Michael, Rachel, Natalie, Kirsten, Andrew, Kelley, Sean, Steph, Stav, Julianne, Michael, and Karine,

with the hope that your generation will impact the world because of a willingness to say "Thank you," "I'm sorry," and "Tell me more."

Contents

CONTENTS

Change the World?

AMANDA, WIDE-EYED AND ECSTATIC, doesn't notice it's 5:47 a.m. but wakes Mom and Dad up. What would you expect from a six-year-old on Christmas morning? Then Grandpa and Grandma arise from sleep amid all the commotion, as does Amanda's brother, Jimmy, and everyone makes their way down to the Christmas tree and the massive number of presents.

With permission granted, Amanda decides to open the big box from her grandparents. Paper flies everywhere, ribbon is tossed aside, and she finally finds the toy she's been asking for since summer. With shouts of excitement, she proceeds to open the box and remove the various pieces.

"What do you say to Grandma and Grandpa?" says Mom. "Thank you," mumbles Amanda, not even turning her head to look at the givers of the gift.

A few hours later in the day, Amanda's emotions have turned from ecstasy to agony. She comes screaming into the kitchen, doubled over in apparent pain. "Jimmy punched me in the stomach," she blurts out between sobs. "Jimmy!"

yells mom. "Come to the kitchen." Jimmy, with an aura of eight-year-old assertiveness, starts speaking before he's even in sight. "But she pushed me first." As Jimmy enters the room, Dad makes him stand in front of Amanda. "What do you say to your sister?" In an almost inaudible voice, with no hint of contrition and an inner conviction that he will do it again given the first opportunity, the words come out: "I'm sorry."

That evening, fifteen-year-old Olivia returns from visiting her dad. It's the first Christmas Day she has spent away from her mom, stepdad, and stepsiblings. Everyone is excited to see her when she arrives, but she has interrupted their board game, so there's little conversation. Mom asks how her time went, and Olivia begins with the usual teenage brevity: "Fine." On his way into the kitchen to get coffee, Dad says, "Tell me more," but Olivia has already gone down the hallway toward her room, and he's in a hurry to get back to the game. Connection missed.

"Thank you."

"I'm sorry."

"Tell me more."

Most of us link these three phrases with good manners. We assume that's their sole purpose. Rearing children to be well-behaved, or at least to appear that way, will come about if they learn to repeat "Thank you," "I'm sorry," and "Tell me more" with frequency.

But what if these three phrases could change the world? With all its challenges, problems, tensions, and difficulties?

Journeying with Others

As moms and dads, we believe that saying "Thank you," "I'm sorry," and "Tell me more" will help our children become better people, friends, partners, employees, neighbors, and global citizens. Manners are a foundation for navigating our connection with others. But we need more than manners.

During elementary school recess, teachers are helping children learn to play with others. High school parents are vigilant in watching their sons' and daughters' relationships. High-quality romantic connections require the ability to interact well. Almost every workplace expects employees to connect well with coworkers, clients, and customers. Living next door to someone from another country, race, or faith is an invitation to be hospitable and engage. Being a congresswoman, senator, president, prime minister, member of parliament, or community advocate offers you the privilege and responsibility to interact helpfully with multiple people.

Can you imagine a world where we didn't need to journey with others?

Some of us do have those fantasies. Feeling the burden of "the other" can be exhausting. A life-withering partner. An energy-consuming child. An exasperating family member. An irritating coworker. A frustrating neighbor. An annoying politician. We would love a world where it was just us. In communion with ourselves and no one else, we wouldn't have to deal with "the other."

The reality, in the nonfantasy world, is different. Every

day people impact us, whether in the home, on the road, at work, or simply watching the news. And we impact others. By what we do and say, as well as by what we *don't* do or say. And we impact each other. The more we pretend we don't have influence on one another, the more deeply entrenched cultural norms keep us from truly seeing one another.

Although manners may be a starting point on the journey of how to relate, the three phrases take on new meaning when you begin to reflect on our daily journey with "the other."

- If we say "Thank you," we're acknowledging the way others impact us.
- If we say "I'm sorry," we're acknowledging the way we impact others.
- If we say "Tell me more," we're acknowledging the way we impact each other.

Think of these three statements as one way to assess the relational quality of journeying with others. How frequently do my wife, daughter, coworkers, and close friends hear me say "Thank you," "I'm sorry," or "Tell me more"? The world is a better place when political, religious, and public-square leaders—and the rest of us—have a way of being that acknowledges others' mutual impact.

Something Is Wrong

At first glance, these three statements are compelling. A world where people frequently said "Thank you," "I'm sorry," and "Tell me more" would be idyllic. Imagine marriages where each partner consistently acknowledged how their mate impacted them, how they impacted their mate, and how they impacted each other. Imagine a political or religious world where all those in power were known for their frequent use of these three phrases. Picture neighborhoods where this was the paradigm that characterized all the relationships down the block and around the corner. International relations would shift markedly if governments and countries had this level of discourse.

Just as manners run the risk of being overly simplistic, so does this basic outline of three phrases. Life doesn't work that way. Some people never say "Thank you" in a way that values the other. And there are those who are known for never saying "Sorry." Many of us have been in relationships where we're always on the receiving end of a self-centered "*I'll* tell *you* more." In the face of these realities, learning to speak these words will hardly change the world. Why?

Entitlement, Victimization, Individualism

Much of Western culture is in the grips of entitlement, victimization, and individualism, with the consequence that it's challenging and countercultural to say "Thank you," "I'm sorry," or "Tell me more."

Entitlement. Newborns are captivating. Cute and adorable, they're the center of attention at Christmas, political rallies, and local malls. Their daily lives are interesting. Food, the sole responsibility of the parents, comes in one end regularly, often on demand. (To translate, "on demand" means screaming, yelling, crying, or some combination of the three.) After due process, the waste comes out the other end, and it's the parents' responsibility to deal with the consequences of that action, one that employs almost all five senses. That process is sometimes on demand as well. A dirty diaper, after all, isn't pleasant for the tiny infant, so he may well scream, yell, or cry. Apart from the odd smile, a lot of sleeping, and a few other "look at what he did" gestures, this is early life for the new baby. He makes demands for special treatment, and his parents oblige.

You can imagine the shock if the two-month-old sat up in his crib and exclaimed, "Thanks so much, Mom. That was an outstanding change. I feel much better now. Feel my gratitude." For developmental reasons, both physical and verbal, we know that wouldn't happen, but we also know it wouldn't occur because infants deserve special treatment. They have a right to be treated that way. Special privileges are appropriate when you are two months old. We don't expect them to say "Thank you," although many parents would value just a little bit of appreciation in those early years.

One of the major problems with many post-infant

people? Life doesn't change all that much. While I may not cry and yell with infant-like expressions, I do the same in more sophisticated and subtle "adult" ways. Sadly, this tendency is frequently reinforced by parents who, having lived the infant years responding on demand to "feed me" or "change me," have continued to cater to the demands and expectations of their older children in such a way that entitlement runs deep.

Outside the home, entitled adults then get exposed to the marketing of a consumerist culture. We learn that we deserve easy credit, loans, homes, holidays, and credit cards. We experience deep disappointment when our perception of what we deserve in our workplace and marriage, what we expect from our mosque, church, or synagogue, and what we want from our politicians don't come to fruition.

At the core of entitlement is a problem with saying "Thank you" because of a high commitment to thinking *I deserve it*. If something is deserved, why would you say "Thank you"?

Victimization. A pivotal moment in debates around the social, legal, moral, and psychological issues related to being sorry and victimization occurred in a 1992 legal case. Stella Liebeck ordered a coffee from a drive-through window at her local McDonald's in Albuquerque, New Mexico. As she pulled the lid off to add cream and sugar, the whole cup of coffee spilled on her lap, burning her to such a degree that she required skin grafting and lengthy rehabilitation. Lawyers took the case on, suing McDonald's for negligence because the coffee was dangerously hot—and at a much higher temperature than how other establishments served coffee. Jury deliberations led to McDonald's being held 80 percent responsible for the burns and Liebeck being held 20 percent responsible.

Some accused Liebeck's lawyers of initiating a frivolous suit, but we can now look back with the perspective of thirty years and realize that this case predicted much of contemporary culture. Even though Stella spilled her coffee because she put it between her knees and took off the lid, a lawsuit with a minute analysis of the temperature of the coffee was appropriate. She wasn't entirely to blame for what happened but was a victim of a fast-food chain. The lawsuit made a poignant point about the allocation of wrong.

Remember Jimmy's response when confronted about the punch to his sister's midsection? "She pushed me first." He's only been on the planet for eight years, but already he's learned to confuse reasons and excuses. Technically he may be right. Amanda did push him, which has given him an apparent reason to respond in kind, although one might wonder whether a punch from an eight-year-old is of the exact nature and quality as a push from his six-year-old sister. But now, he's taken the reason and converted it into an excuse: "Why would you punish me, Dad, when I was a victim of the push?"

It's straightforward to move into the space of the victim. The social sciences have helped us frame the present in light of the past, and we're in a cultural moment where what's "wrong" is up for discussion. *I'm not responsible because of this or that*, this line of thinking goes, *so why would I say "I'm sorry"?*

"I know you struggle to deal with my anger," says the father to his daughter, "but you need to understand that it comes up because of my historical sense of being marginalized." "I know I hurt you by having multiple affairs," says the husband to his wife, "but I made a mistake, and a lot of it is due to my underlying need for affection." The mathematical equation is explicit—

marginalization = anger + abuse of others.

Or

need for affection = multiple affairs + hurting spouse.

If that's where the angry father and the unfaithful spouse stay, they'll display classic victimization. They bear little responsibility for their influence on others and have no sense they need to say "I'm sorry." Someone, or something, else is to blame.

While "Thank you" acknowledges others have impacted us, "I'm sorry" reflects an awareness that we have impacted others. It's the opposite of "It's not my fault." Blame shifting and converting reasons into excuses gets us off the hook. We can spill our coffee, hit our sibling, be angry with our children, cheat on our spouse, and justify and legitimize what we did by holding people or circumstances responsible. In the process, we fail to acknowledge the experience of the other, and they never hear "I'm sorry."

Individualism. I once taught an introductory counseling course in Africa. One day a student asked, "So you are telling us that in North America, when people have a problem, they meet an individual stranger, who may be younger than them, in an office and pay them money for advice?" If you've had much cross-cultural experience, you'll understand the predicament. Part of you wants to say, "Yes, what's the problem with that?" but then you dread that your Western bias isn't shared everywhere, and you know that the teacher is about to become a student.

"What do you do here if you have a problem?" I asked.

She responded, "We go to the town center and meet with a group of elders in a circle. The youngest one speaks first and the oldest one speaks last as we go around the circle sharing opinions. We believe that community is key in our healing."

That interaction and many others since have made me acutely aware of the difference between seeing people as part of a community versus seeing them as individuals. In the West, being true to ourselves has become a virtue, and we prize privacy, self-direction, and independence. And now we have an entire industry helping us do self-care, as the individualism project has left us with wounds and warts.

The title of Sherry Turkle's book *Alone Together: Why We Expect More from Technology and Less from Each Other*, captures our current predicament all too well. We have unprecedented access to information. Connecting with people instantly in any part of the world is straightforward. So-called friends are accessible to us through multiple technological devices. But we are alone. Our sense of community seems to be decreasing as our experience of isolation and loneliness increases.

Let's return to our opening story for an example of how being alone together can affect us. As Olivia participates in her blended family, she has her own internal experience. Her biological dad is off with someone else, she has a new stepdad and two new stepsiblings, and her mom is in a different marriage. Her first Christmas with her dad (and away from everyone else) was filled with various emotions. Some of them were positive, but there was sadness and not a little anger. When she says "Fine," in response to "How'd it go?" what she means is "I'm still processing it myself." When her stepdad says "Tell me more," that's the correct phrase but the wrong time because he was more interested in his drink and the board game.

But who's going to hear Olivia's story? Given all that she's going through, she needs human interaction, preferably face-to-face, where someone says, "I hear you spent your first Christmas with your dad since your parents split. Tell me more." Conversations of this nature—where stories are shared and experiences exchanged—seem less frequent these days. In the high pace of a culture that prizes individualism, we can easily stay distant from one another and communicate that "my story matters most."

Many of us are paying consultants, trainers, coaches, mentors, counselors, spiritual directors, and the like to help us improve, support us in accomplishing a goal, and provide input as we deal with challenges. I suspect an underlying dynamic driving these legitimate pursuits is *finding places where someone will listen to our stories.* Where someone will ask us to tell them more. Going to various counselors has been a positive experience for me, but there's no question that one of the most powerful aspects of these interactions was that someone wanted to hear my story. "Tell me more" was a welcome invitation.

While "Thank you" acknowledges others have impacted us, and "I'm sorry" reflects an awareness that we have impacted others, "Tell me more" is an affirmation that we impact each other. But we have to deal with the cultural hurdles of entitlement, victimization, and individualism in using these phrases.

Coping with Culture

There are three ways to cope with cultural trends: fight, succumb, or embody.

Fight. You know the fighters. Some are in your family. Your church. Your workplace. Always decrying the "way things are." Everyone is entitled. Victimization is killing us. Do you remember the good old days when we had community and neighborhood, not all this individualistic navel-gazing?

The "fight them" approach demonizes others as wrong and ironically makes the observers seem arrogant, apparently untouched by the culture they're criticizing. The style of their evaluative sermons, talks, books, and articles isn't a compelling alternative. Their way of fighting the bad is as bad as the bad they are fighting.

German philosopher Friedrich Nietzsche captures the potential danger in this approach:

> He who fights with monsters should look to it that he himself does not become a monster. And when you gaze long into an abyss the abyss also gazes into you.[1]

Succumb. The succumbing crowd pays little attention to the way the culture influences them. They participate in entitlement, victimization, and individualism almost unknowingly. We often see this with those in positions of power. Disappointing to the rest of us, who expect more from our political, religious, and workplace leaders, those in charge seem like everyone else, participating in a way of being that doesn't involve treating "the other" well.

This tendency may be most evident in the left–right political tensions. Ironically, both sides claim to be correct and see the other as a significant threat. There's little interest in the common good or care for the other, no sense of gratitude for the opposition; there's only a belief that the other side victimizes my side. In many ways, both the right and the left have succumbed to a way of being that keeps the articulation of "Thank you," "I'm sorry," and "Tell me more" to a minimum.

Embody. A third option, an alternative that doesn't involve fighting or succumbing, is embodying a counter-cultural lifestyle, choosing to function differently than the majority around us. The ethos we bring to our way of being can offer a winsome and refreshing alternative to the aggressiveness of fighting or the passivity of succumbing.

In living a life where our attitude and words express . . .

- "Thank you," we bring an attitude of gratitude in a culture of entitlement.
- "I'm sorry," we bring an attitude of remorse in a culture of victimization.
- "Tell me more," we bring an attitude of care in a culture of individualism.

If we walked with everyone, whomever they are, others would experience our gratitude, remorse, and care. Gratitude would move to the center, while entitlement moved to the edge. Maximizing remorse would minimize victimization. Care would become primary, while individualism would become secondary.

Elegance of Simplicity

Three short phrases. A total of eight words. Seem simplistic? How could their repetition change the world? Dangers present themselves when we rush to trite and clichéd phrases. Sometimes our leaders, both religious and political, resort to this overly basic approach. Everyone knows the world has way more complexity than a spiritual quote or a political byline.

My office window faces an inlet where international cargo ships arrive from various parts of the world and are unloaded in our local port. These massive vessels are close to 700 feet long and have a volume of space available for cargo, fuel, and crew of 22,790 tonnes (measured in Gross Registered Tonnage) and a fuel capacity of up to 800,000 gallons. While crossing the Pacific Ocean is facilitated by their impressive magnitude, the journey through the inlet and the eventual arrival at the dock is made possible by a much smaller boat. Tugboats, close to 90 feet long, with a GRT of 441 and a fuel capacity of 26,000 gallons, facilitate the journey's final leg.[2] The imposing and extraordinary are expertly and gently guided by the small and nimble.

Just as tugboats point larger vessels in a particular direction, these three phrases perform a similar function. Their usage embodies an alternative way of being to a culture moving in a different direction. More gratitude, remorse, and care will make for a better arrival at the dock.

CULTURE SAYS	ATTITUDE	WE SAY	ATTITUDE
"I deserve it."	entitlement	"Thank you."	gratitude
"It's not my fault."	victimization	"I'm sorry."	remorse
"My story matters most."	individualism	"Tell me more."	care

Importance of Why

If we believe that gratitude, remorse, and care matter, we do so because these things agree with our underlying principles. There's a reason that these three phrases matter. There's always a *why* undergirding and inspiring "Thank you," "I'm sorry," and "Tell me more."

Many people in contemporary culture have an ethic of treating people well. That's their big story. As they move in and out of their home, workplace, and relationships, they do their best to be responsive to others, and their goal in saying these three phrases is an underlying commitment to the fair treatment of people.

Others might have a big story rooted in secular humanism. People are seen as self-reliant and self-sufficient, able to determine their direction without reference to a deity or an otherworldly god. At times this is expressed as atheism (where there's a complete absence of belief in God) or agnosticism (where there's a belief that God isn't or can't be known). There's no question that 16 percent of the world's population who adhere to these philosophies could easily adopt and act on the three phrases in response to the *why* question because they take humanity seriously.

Eastern religions like Confucianism, Buddhism, Taoism, Hinduism, and Sikhism comprise about 24 percent of the world's population and generally differ from Western religions because followers worship multiple gods rather than one God. Adherents of these religions have a big story, a *why* behind the *what*. Worship of the gods also includes appropriate relationships with people.

The three main religions that trace their origins back to Abraham—Judaism, Islam, and Christianity—comprise 54 percent of the world's population. Each has a big story embedded in a sacred text that outlines core beliefs and expected behaviors toward God and others.[3]

For Jews, the Tanakh (or Hebrew Scriptures) and the Talmud, a collection of writings from rabbis, emphasize that one's relationship with God and the other is crucial.

The Koran and commentary from Muhammad and his followers in the Hadith provide Muslims with instruction on their relationship with Allah and people.

Christians build their life on adherence to the Holy Bible, comprising Old and New Testaments, with its dual emphasis on relating to God and others.

As a Christian who finds his identity in God, I believe that my relationship with people flows directly from that connection. That doesn't mean I have to speak Bible, not English, to people. Nor does it mean that I have to push all my conversations with others toward religious or spiritual matters. Instead, peoples' experience of me should be one of gratitude, remorse, and care.

When Jesus was asked how best to summarize all the commandments, his response was arresting: *Love God. Love others.* For followers of Jesus, these two commands are inseparable, and they pull the Christian faith together. How we relate to others flows from our relationship with God. Love is the action. People are the recipients. Expressing "Thank you," "I'm sorry," and "Tell me more" to people is putting words to love: *I see you. I notice you. We impact each other.* For Jesus, loving God but not loving others is the ultimate contradiction.

People who know me should frequently hear me say "Thank you," "I'm sorry," and "Tell me more." They should sense that I'm not a Christian who is continually fighting a culture of entitlement, victimization, and individualism, nor am I someone who has succumbed to the intoxicating nature of that culture. I seek to be a person who embodies an alternative story, and others should be beneficiaries of that choice.

At the end of the book, I'll provide more detailed personal reflections. For now, it's enough to state that I want gratitude, remorse, and care to characterize all people, especially those who identify as Christian. I fear that isn't the message we're offering at this moment in time. We have lost our gratefulness, see everyone else as wrong, and are more interested in having others listen to our stories than in listening to theirs. We've become known for our stand on sociocultural issues, political affiliation, voting preferences, and locating ourselves on the nebulous left–right continuum. And even as we hold to some of these commitments, we seem to be consistently marginalizing the other by our less-than-exemplary attitudes and actions, rather than welcoming what they offer.

Perspective

This book calls for increased gratitude, remorse, and care, but we need a proper perspective on *how* and *when*.

Gratitude is a mindset that should characterize our general way of being. Still, to suggest that every circumstance should be an occasion for saying "Thank you" is inhumane. It would be absurd, for example, to suggest that Amanda should thank Jimmy for punching her. It would be appropriate, however, for Amanda to live with an overall perspective of gratitude for her relationship with her brother. You can be thankful in a circumstance without being grateful for it.

A person who is always apologizing for any and every action isn't expressing genuine remorse but carries a perpetual weight of guilt that's out of proportion to individual events. But someone who never takes responsibility for the negative influence of their behavior has also lost perspective. How and when to express "I'm sorry" isn't always straightforward.

Gratitude and remorse are conditional, offered in a way that's suitable to the circumstance. "Tell me more" requires a different perspective. Asking someone to tell us more is a conscious choice that's always available to us. It rarely, if ever, has any conditions. Offering someone "Tell me more" is a gift without qualification.

Invitation to Engage

Let me extend an invitation to you—an invitation to engage.

A massive amount of information, a considerable amount of conflict, and deep disappointment in leadership, politics, religious systems, organizational structures, economic equity, and environmental care characterizes this cultural moment. In response, techniques and strategies are proposed, individuals offer themselves as the solution, various concepts and ideas are discussed, and political affiliations are promoted. But when it is all said and done, we may need to get back to basics.

With the other as our primary focus, we need to *cultivate an attitude expressed in a life and lifestyle* that communicates gratitude, remorse, and care, as we pay careful attention to the *why* question, determining the big story underlying our little stories. I invite you to engage in the rest of the book with this in mind.

I don't want to minimize the importance of concepts, but the rest of the book is low on concepts and high on stories. We need more stories. Telling stories has the advantage that they almost always elicit other stories. So, as you read, don't just get caught up in these stories but think about your own story. Let my stories be a springboard to reflecting on your own experiences. What have you learned about gratitude, remorse, and care in your lifetime? How might you create new stories of this type in the future?

I also don't want to minimize the importance of information, but the rest of the book is low on information and high on wisdom. We need more wisdom. Wisdom puts the "if . . . then . . ." of life together. If we engage in a particular action, there will be a consequence. A different result will flow from another action. Every behavior has an outcome. As you read, reflect on the wisdom statement at the end of the section by looking backward and forward. Where have you learned this wisdom in the past, either through success or failure? How might you bring this wisdom to future circumstances?

I want to engage these three phrases more thoughtfully. I want to express them more frequently. I want a lifestyle that embodies them, and I desire the same experience for you. The world can change.

Part One

Thank You

WHEN CICERO, the philosopher-statesman from the century before Christ's birth, spoke these words in a speech, he provided an aspiration that needs to characterize all of us.

> I wish to be adorned with every virtue, yet there is nothing which I can esteem more highly than being and appearing grateful. For this one virtue is not only the greatest, but is also the parent of all the other virtues.[1]

Being and appearing grateful is the ultimate virtue, the parent that births all other admirable virtues.

Rooted in the Latin word *gratus*, which means pleasing or thankful, gratitude is an acknowledgment and appreciation experience. It's our way of saying, "You've done something, said something, or just been who you are, and I'm grateful. I want to acknowledge you and the impact you've had on me."

Psychologists argue that gratitude is both a state of mind and a personality trait. Traits are qualities that are embedded in who we are. Having a gratitude trait means that you're

23

attentive to situations where you've been the recipient of something deserving of appreciation and that you respond accordingly. It is who you are. Can you think of someone for whom gratitude comes easily? That person embodies gratitude as a quality, a trait. Can you think of acquaintances, work colleagues, and family members who never seem to "get it" when it comes to expressing gratefulness? That is a trait deficit.

The state of gratitude is the experience of thankfulness in the moment. When the clerk gives us a receipt in the grocery store and we say, "Thank you," that may not reveal a personality characteristic of gratitude; it may be simply a way to respond at the time. It is more something I do rather than who I am.

In the last twenty years, social-science literature has begun to link gratitude with a vast array of personal benefits. Those who express more gratitude tend to be more agreeable, open, optimistic, and happy, experience better sleep and mood, and have less inflammation, stress, depression, and anxiety. You could summarize this research by saying that thanking others is good for you![2]

Cicero links gratitude with *virtue*—attributes that are good, right, true, and beautiful. This is distinct from personality, momentary states, or the personal benefits that accrue to us from thanking others. The practice of virtue is rooted in something much more profound than a personality style. If we say "Thank you" at the grocery store, we may or may not be exhibiting a virtue. But when the virtue of gratitude is deeply resident within us, grocery-store clerks will be included in our world of thank-yous.

Virtue isn't concerned with the outcome. I don't express gratitude because it will be good for me or bring me benefits. Virtues are themselves good. Appropriate. Moral. Ethical.

Gratitude is an acknowledgment of the other. They are in view. They are the focus. Genuine virtue is probably missing if a personal benefit is the focus of gratitude.

As a Christian, I want to embrace the virtue of gratitude. I don't want my thank-yous to be dependent on circumstances or only spoken when I'm in situations that seem to warrant this reaction. I don't want to be absorbed by the positive benefits that will come my way if I'm grateful.

Instead, I want to understand, cultivate, and practice the virtue of gratitude. Recognizing my life is a gift from God, I experience thankfulness, and so, in turn, I want to watch out for others who impact me positively and express my appreciation to them. My gratitude for God's gifts becomes the *why* behind my thank-you. And in case I get entangled with *I deserve it* entitlement, where I ignore gratitude for others, I keep reminding myself that the giving God is also a merciful God who regularly gives me what I don't deserve. I want to do the same for everyone else in my life.

It can be tempting to fight the entitlement culture or succumb to its influence. I want to embody an alternative story.

What follows are twenty stories on gratitude followed by a simple statement of wisdom. They capture scenarios where I learned the importance of saying "Thank you," sometimes from what I or others did well and other times from my failures or others' shortcomings. Some of these stories describe experiences in the home, others relate to community engagement, and some originate in the workplace.

When we listen to other people's stories, we stimulate our imaginations and deepen our curiosity. As you read these stories, pause and ponder. Read through them slowly. Think of your own story and the degree to which it resonates with mine. Do you prefer a particular approach to gratitude from these stories? What does that look like for you? How might you pursue it?

Ponder the wisdom statements. Note the linkage of behavior and consequences, actions and outcome. How has this worked out in your life? Do you aspire to a different coupling of what you do and how things turn out? Spend time bathing in the wisdom, allowing it to wash over you and soak in.

As you read, imagine what the world would be like if we said "Thank you" to express gratitude in a culture that says "I deserve it" to express entitlement.

Whiny Space

COMPLAINING DOESN'T END IN INFANCY. If you don't believe me, go to a mall and listen carefully.

Infants are making odd, whistle-like sounds. Three-year-olds are being dragged, literally, out of a store with a loud and pathetic "But I *want* it." Teens sitting in the food court are griping about someone and what they have done. Couples, with hushed tones, are sniping at each other about how long they've been in the store. Older men drinking Italian coffee are waxing eloquent about increased income tax.

Complaining is an expression of legitimate dissatisfaction with the hope of resolution. Venting, in contrast, is a complaint without hope of resolution. The term *whining*, which started as a description of a hissing sound and could be used of both people and animals, became known as a feeble or immature way of complaining. The whiner is an excessive complainer.

Many families and workplaces have a sprinkling of whiners. Often their original complaint was legitimate and well-founded. They weren't treated well. Mistakes were made. But whiners often can't move on. Whether their initial claim was addressed or not, whining is their way of being in the world.

Not only do venters and whiners create weariness for those around them but evidence suggests that these people's brains get rewired over time. Eventually, the whiner can look at any situation, positive or negative, and end up in a whiny space.[1]

In the workplace, I've noticed that those who specialize in excessive complaining are usually the same people who are very low on verbalized gratitude. When they speak up in staff meetings, you know it'll be on the complaining-venting-whining scale, and it's a challenge to figure out which of the three is dominating. Rarely, if ever, do they express thanks to people, because in their world, people and communities always fall short.

I wonder what would happen if those who invariably live in this space were to see the other not as the cause of their problems or the dumping ground for their perpetual criticisms but as someone worthy of appreciation. Gratitude is an excellent ointment for the abrasion of excessive complaints.

Pause and Reflect

If we see others as worthy of appreciation, gratitude will increase as complaining lessens.

Hakarat Hatov

WHEN PEOPLE LEAVE a relationship, their fundamental approach to gratitude is often revealed.

Rose-colored-glasses types act as if the departing person had done nothing wrong. A fantastic person who did everything well and always made perfect decisions. Like my own sunglasses, which make the sky and ocean much bluer than they are, this overly optimistic perspective may say more about the observer than the observed.

Others assess the departing person negatively. Nothing was done well. The relationship was lacking, their attitude was suspect, and they weren't appreciated. I call these people "nightshade types." Because our bedroom is quite bright in the morning, I wear nightshades to block out the light. As a result, everything I "see" is dark.

The all-bad or all-good viewpoint on the departed shows up when employees leave, bosses quit, relationships sour, marriages terminate, and even when people die. In the process, people reveal their perspective on gratitude.

If my spouse leaves or there's a breach in a family

relationship and I'm a nightshade type, it's easy for me to see nothing worthy of gratitude.

If I'm speaking at the funeral of someone many people disliked and I'm expressing thankfulness for everything about him, people will question the genuineness of my gratitude.

How do we cut through the allure of excessive pessimism or extreme optimism?

I love how the literal Hebrew renders the concept of gratitude—*hakarat hatov*, which means recognizing the good. In Jewish thought, there are three components to this phrase. We are to acknowledge the good done to us, bring optimism to what we observe, and express gratitude to the other.

In other words, when bosses leave, relationships fracture, or marriages disintegrate, we engage in an internal process of recognition. What was the good that was done to me or for me? That can only happen if we bring thoughtful optimism to what we observe, an understanding that despite the tension, difficulty, and even disappointment, there's good to be found. But it's not enough to note the good internally; gratitude then needs to be expressed to the other.

I wonder if our struggle with gratitude reflects a problem with noting the good in every person and circumstance.

Pause and Reflect

If we recognize the good in others, gratitude will replace excessive optimism or extreme pessimism.

Taken for Granted

IT WAS MY SECOND DAY in the hospital after a heart attack. Pushing a stretcher, the orderly came in and said I was going down for X-rays. I protested mildly, suggesting that I could easily walk. The response was non-negotiable: I was going on the stretcher.

We went down the cardiac ward, with people doing what I always do in hospitals, looking down at me with a slightly concerned look or a reassuring smile. Some of them, no doubt wondering about the severity of my heart issues. Then the wait for the elevator, where numerous people were poised for their journey up or down. All of them standing. Vertical.

Often these trips were on special elevators, but this time I was with the public. All of them standing, looking down. The lengthy hallway led to the radiology department, where many of us in the horizontal position were parked along nondescript walls.

And all I could see was a ceiling. Bland in décor with excessively bright fluorescent lights, the ceiling loomed large.

It was my vista. Life took on a whole new perspective, and I didn't like it.

I'd never thought of life in terms of being horizontal or vertical until that morning. Vertical became a symbol of being well, able, healthy, self-sufficient. Horizontal reflected sickness, frailty, dependence, vulnerability.

I thought of my days before the heart attack. I had been healthy, rested, stress-free, loving my work. I was now horizontal, in a hospital. What flooded my emotions in that horizontal position, on that stretcher, looking at that ceiling, was gratitude, with a tinge of guilt.

How great is it to be healthy? To be able to walk down a hallway. Push the button at the elevator. To be in a vertical position and see others eye to eye. These were the signs of well-being. And I didn't have them.

I wonder how many of us are in a relationship, job, home, neighborhood, or situation where we're taking it all for granted and having trouble saying "Thank you" before the loss.

Pause and Reflect

If we lose something we've taken for granted, we are provided with a fresh opportunity to be thankful.

Being Specific

ON A RECENT PLANE TRIP, I noted a change in the usual end-of-flight announcement. "Thank you for flying with us today. We know that you could have chosen another airline, so we appreciate you selecting us."

For years I've heard the standard "Thank you for flying with us" with no specificity about why these flight attendants were grateful. I could surmise that my choice of that airline brought them more business and greater economic stability. But the new announcement acknowledged something real. When we go on a trip that involves a flight, we all choose between multiple airlines. We expend time and energy selecting one carrier, and by implication, we don't choose others. The new announcement acknowledged this reality by providing gratitude with specificity.

When I think about gratitude that I've received, I note that I'm more influenced by words that capture the detail of *how* I've influenced others.

Because I do a lot of public speaking, I frequently hear "Thank you," "Appreciated that," "Thanks for being here."

Such expressions are always appreciated and valued, and like everyone else, I find them much more reassuring than "I disagree with your premise" or "I didn't understand what you were getting at."

By far, the best expressions of gratitude for speakers go along these lines: "Thank you. I appreciate the way you take complex subjects and make them simple but not simplistic. I not only see where you are going when you explain things but I understand the implications. Thank you."

Not only does this feedback provide affirmation, it also sets us up nicely for the following speaking event. We have more clarity on how we process and explain ideas and link them with the audience's lived experience. Gratitude in the moment becomes inspirational in the future.

If we move beyond only saying "Thank you" and offer rich detail, we not only provide others with more encouragement but set them up to continue to work on their strengths.

Pause and Reflect

If we express gratitude with specificity, others will understand how they've impacted us.

Ignoring Roles

PEOPLE WHO CLEAN TOILETS are usually at the bottom of the hierarchy. Whether they're in an airport, theater, library, restaurant, school, factory, or company, their task is perceived as menial. Their status is considered low.

This work revolves around a piece of hardware that is the conduit between eliminating human waste and its disposal into a sewage system. In so-called developed countries, this entire process is kept hidden. The act of elimination is usually a closed-door experience, and very few of us understand the mechanics of sewage treatment.

In many countries, those tasked with cleaning toilets are poor immigrants who can't find other work. Toilet cleaners don't get paid a lot, and probably no one grows up dreaming about cleaning toilets as their occupational choice.

I've noticed that when I see a toilet cleaner at work, it's easy to turn away, both literally and symbolically. With an "I guess someone needs to do it" attitude, I would prefer to ignore their work and, in the process, negate them, as well.

Better to treat them with the same level of secrecy that characterizes the whole process.

Then I met Alex.

After moving to a new organization, I was intrigued by Alex, the toilet cleaner. As we got to know each other, I heard his attitudes and motivation for his work. He saw himself as playing a role in the overall organizational system, and there was dignity in the way he carried out his responsibilities. Not surprisingly, it led me to regularly thank him for what he was doing and what he brought to it.

Alex has helped me be on the lookout for those in roles that could be seen as lesser. Ushers at sports and entertainment events. Street sweepers who clean up after parades. Ticket takers at movie theaters. Every system has them. I have thanked more toilet cleaners in the last ten years than in my whole life.

I wonder what would happen if all of us, but particularly those in leadership, gifted those in so-called lesser roles with the dignity of conversation and a genuine expression of thanks.

Pause and Reflect

If we verbalize gratitude to those in so-called lesser roles, we value their actions and affirm who they are.

Fearful Gratitude

GRATITUDE IS NOT UNLIKE ALCOHOL. In moderation, it can be positive, but too much of it may reveal underlying problems.

I was once in a leadership role where a person in the organization was continually expressing gratitude. They thanked me for everything and anything. With regularity.

You can get lulled into this kind of fawning and like it. It's attractive when someone constantly tells you that they are thankful for who you are and what you do. But after a while, I found it tiresome. I began to doubt his authenticity and wondered whether his regular thank-yous said more about him than about how well I was functioning.

As it turned out, he struggled with deep shame. He carried around the burden of thinking *There's something wrong with me*, so he read all his relationships through that grid. And when he was with someone who was in authority over him, the shame deepened, his sense of self was lacking, and he found it easy to extol the virtues of a boss. Lurking behind all this was not an appreciation of the other but deep fear.

Fear of what I, as a leader, might do to him, the lowly staff member.

It's ironic how nice we can be when we're living in fear. I've noticed that when I'm with a dog that scares me, I tend to say "Nice doggy" while I'm patting her head. But when I'm with a dog that doesn't scare me, I don't speak the same way. In the presence of fear, I fawn over the dog and over-value her because I'm worried about myself. I don't believe it's a lovely doggy, but I express appreciation because I'm afraid of what she might do to me.

At its best, gratitude is a genuine expression of thanks for the other and reflects an attitude of wanting to acknowledge the good that comes from them. When I express excessive gratitude, I am probably most concerned about myself.

Pause and Reflect

If we aren't overwhelmed by a fear of others, our expression of gratitude will be genuine.

Communal Merit

MERIT IS A SLIPPERY WORD. On the one hand, it describes something we are worthy of or deserve. An award of merit in an athletic competition signals that we've earned recognition because of our high performance. But we can become pre-occupied with credit and feel entitled to it. Then it becomes a right, and we tend to negate others' influence and lack gratitude.

Many speeches at the Oscars and other award shows illustrate the opposite tendency. Recipients start with "I have a lot of people to thank." As they go through the lengthy list, it's clear that they don't perceive their success as solely a reflection of their own energy, expertise, and effort. Instead, a community of contributors have each played a role. They've helped cultivate success and resultant merit and are now deserving of gratitude.

Many of the roots of merit can be traced to the world of education. From our very early years in school, learning is connected to grades and graduation. If you don't learn, you won't get good grades, and you won't graduate. Many of us still have visceral reactions to the word *failure* and deep hunger for "success" because of this early exposure to a merit-based system.

As we move into the workplace, other variables are substituted for grades and graduation. What's my job title? How many people work for me? What's my salary? How significant is my influence? Worth and value become tied to status and power.

We've all known people who are obsessed with their merit. They see themselves as having achieved greatness, and their spirit of self-congratulation is such that they see themselves as totally responsible for what they've achieved. They're the self-made woman or man deserving all the credit. (Or so they think.)

In contrast, others recognize that through various seasons of their lives, they have been aided, counseled, guided, mentored, taught, and coached by a variety of people who have played a significant role in whatever merit they've achieved. This spirit of self-forgetfulness doesn't lead them to see merit as a right but rather as something others have fostered.

It may well be that gratitude would increase if we allowed our merit to be a communal enterprise.

Pause and Reflect

If we see merit as communal, we'll express appreciation for the positive impact of others.

All About Me

AS POPULIST POLITICS has risen in the early part of the twenty-first century, more leaders are being analyzed psychologically. Their detractors have diagnosed a number of them with NPD—narcissistic personality disorder.[1]

In the diagnostic world, someone with NPD has an inflated sense of their own importance, achievements, and abilities, requires excessive attention and admiration, and operates relationally with entitlement rather than empathy. Arrogance and anger combine in response to those who don't make them feel superior or give them the praise they deserve. Rage, contempt, and belittling are not uncommon in how this is expressed.

Sadly, while those who battle NPD look arrogant and pretentious on the surface, their underlying feelings are often characterized by insecurity, shame, vulnerability, and humiliation, usually rooted in unhealthy family-of-origin dynamics.

As is true with many psychiatric assessments, particular NPD symptoms may show up in the way all of us relate to others, even when the formal diagnosis doesn't apply.

When I'm in an arrogant and angry space, I find my relationships are problematic. Wallowing in an "it's all about me" perspective, I become preoccupied with how others treat me and whether they're meeting my expectations. Inevitably that arrogance turns to anger because others aren't doing what I want and need.

Maybe you have a colleague, family member, friend, or political leader who has a personality disorder characterized by narcissism or who leans this way at certain times. You know what it's like to be on the receiving end of arrogance and anger. You, the other, become responsible for the fact they aren't being treated well. You aren't feeding their deep sense of entitlement.

Anger and arrogance are a deadly mix when laced with self-preoccupation and an approach to the other as a threat, enemy, or competitor. Notable by its absence is gratitude. At best, "Thank you" will be infrequent, and at worst, it'll be completely stifled. What would you expect? The other is there simply to build up an inflated sense of importance. (Or so the narcissist believes.)

It may well be that the presence or absence of gratitude is a symptom of the presence or absence of arrogance and anger.

Pause and Reflect

If we live with a commitment to the other, it won't be all about us, and thank-yous will be frequent.

Obligation Meets Entitlement

IN OUR DATING YEARS, my wife (Bev) and I made vocational and economic decisions that set us on a trajectory that didn't lead to being fabulously wealthy.

When we bought our first house, I believed that we'd get significant monetary help from my parents. This belief wasn't based on something they said.

The situation was straightforward, as I saw it. My parents had more money than we did, so they were required to carry out this responsibility. And because we had made certain decisions, we deserved this special treatment. The reward for making downwardly mobile financial decisions was an influx of cash from parents. A simple *if-then* proposition dominated. If we made such a noble lifestyle choice, then my parents should get with the program.

[their] obligation + [my] entitlement = money

When they gave us an interest-free loan with no timeline for repayment, I remember being overwhelmed with a lack of gratitude. What? A loan? *If you can afford to loan us the money*, I thought, *why don't you just give it to us?*

I remember my experience of frustration at my parents for not fulfilling what I saw as their obligation. It was easy to blame them, see it as their fault, and link my irritation with their behavior. As a result, my lack of gratitude was seemingly legitimized. They didn't do what they were supposed to do, so why would they receive appreciation?

When we construct narratives in our head that combine an entitled "I deserve it" perspective with a "You should _____" obligation, it's vital to confront the assumptions embedded in both. When Bev and I decided to live a certain way, that choice didn't lead to any guarantee of privileges or special treatment. And since my parents weren't participants in that decision, the idea they should contribute significantly to our housing costs reflects a questionable presumption.

Our internally constructed stories about entitlement and obligation have led to a mindset where we've become irritated with so many others and, in the process, rarely express gratitude.

Pause and Reflect

If we practice gratitude, our relationships will be protected from entitlement and unreasonable expectations.

Intoxicating Power

I WAS SITTING in a fancy restaurant with Saul, an impeccably dressed business owner, his self-importance and sense of power showing up in everything he said and did. When we arrived, his treatment of the waiter who showed us to our table was dismissive. On the status ladder, he was many rungs below Saul.

When the menu and water glasses were placed in front of us, Saul received them from the young woman as if she were a robot. He placed his order in a stern, almost demanding way, and his specific instructions on the wine were patronizing. The arrival of the meal brought the same kind of attitude. Disrespectful. Uninterested. Almost demeaning.

Even though we were sitting on simple chairs on a flat floor around the table, it was as if Saul were on a high throne and the restaurant staff were his depersonalized servants doing his bidding. They were beneath him. Not just literally but metaphorically. They couldn't reach up to him. And he wasn't going to reach down to them. Weirdly, it was as if they weren't there. Saul was in a bubble, and they were hidden from view.

Given his status, he was above the wait staff by many standards. But what intrigued me most was the absence of gratitude. He didn't thank anyone for anything. No one's service was acknowledged. Saul was the center of the universe, and those around him were there to not only feed him a meal but also feed his sense of entitlement.

In a culture where there's a lot of talk about money and sex, we need to talk more about power. When power is taken too seriously, we think in hierarchical terms. Some are at the top; others are at the bottom. Some are in charge; others are there to serve those who are in charge. Those in power are deserving and entitled, and others are there to ensure those needs are met. And what's missing when we buy into this mindset? Gratitude.

Pause and Reflect

If we carry our power lightly, we won't hesitate to express gratitude to those who have less power.

Suspicious of Others

I SPENT THE SUMMERS of my late teens and early twenties working in a dairy. Lunchroom conversations centered around three topics—sex, alcohol, and management. The sexual prowess and drinking capacity of my coworkers were impressive and intimidating. At least as they described it. But the big topic? Management.

People in management were people to fear. Suspicion reigned, and fear was in every conversation. Bosses had no care for the workers. Probably making a lot of money themselves, their interest in our wages was negligible. And what did they do anyway? They were always in meetings discussing something, and there was no chance we'd benefit from their deliberations.

What struck me was how the few influenced the many. A couple of my colleagues would get into their management tirade, and it would cultivate an atmosphere where a lot of us were focused on "the management," as if they had no names, lives, faces, or good intent.

Decades later, I've seen this pattern repeated in various

workplaces. Fear and suspicion reign, and nothing good can come from those higher up.

Gratitude is notable only by its absence. And it makes sense. If we live in fear and suspicion of others, how can they affect us positively?

Fear and suspicion are usually rooted in historical, lived experiences. We learn that people aren't to be trusted, that they may not have our best interests at heart or that they pose a significant threat. Often those assessments are accurate and appropriate given what has transpired.

Problems ensue when that legitimate response to particular events and people is carried into other relationships and circumstances. Fear and suspicion no longer become a healthy reaction to real threats; they now wash over all our interactions. The popular acronym for fear—false evidence appearing real—is apt.

I wonder what would happen if we could begin to learn that many people in our current circumstances are positively disposed toward us. This journey might start by learning to express gratitude.

Pause and Reflect

If we notice others' capacity to influence us positively, our suspicion of them will fade and our appreciation will be focused.

Being and Doing

IN WORKING WITH WEALTHY DONORS, as a fundraiser, counselor, and consultant, it has been interesting to find out that many of them experience a lack of appreciation for who they are. Because they have financial resources and a capacity to give, that becomes the preoccupation of individuals and organizations requesting their money. Who they are seems irrelevant.

When I asked a man why he thought he was asked to serve on a nonprofit board, he said, through tears, "My wife has made a lot of money, but everyone knows she would be a terrible board member, so they've asked me. They think that's how they'll get at the money."

I know many wealthy people who try to keep a low profile, avoiding certain events and locations. They know it will not be a "know and be known" occasion but rather an opportunity to be treated like a cash machine.

In the nonprofit charity world, it's not uncommon for staff to believe that what they're doing is the biggest and the best thing. One of my friends calls this "worthy-cause thinking." People can become so impressed with themselves and their charity that they think all they need is money, so they go out and find it.

This is a deadly combination: donors who feel isolated and misunderstood, treated as if all they have to offer is their cash, and charities who need money and show interest in the donor only so they can get some.

There is value in thanking a donor for their gift. When you've given money to a person or organization, it's good to know that they value the money that's come their way. But when you express appreciation for *who they are*—the values that undergirded their gift and their spirit of generosity—the experience is different.

Gratitude for who you are is more impactful than appreciation for what you do. I wonder if, if we fully understood the difference between "being" and "doing," we'd realize the importance of both in expressing thanks to others.

Pause and Reflect

If we strive to see people as whole persons, they experience our gratitude long before they do anything for us.

Ungrateful Consumers

WHEN YOU ANSWER THE PHONE around suppertime and a stranger greets you as if you are best buds, you know what is coming—a sales pitch.

On one such occasion, it was my internet service provider with a special offer. (Why do they always put "special" in front of "offer"? I've never heard of a mundane offer.)

With a slight boost in monthly payment amount, our internet speed could increase. A passionate, enthusiastic offer was made, followed by the typical pause for a positive response.

"I'm happy with my internet speed," I replied.

In the deafening silence, I sensed the stranger looking through his various scripts for the "this is what you say when they say that" lines. Not finding anything, he repeated the pitch verbatim. I, in turn, gave the same response.

Instantly he proceeded to the following overture. For another small outlay of money, I could have over two hundred channels on my TV. When I responded, "I have a full-time job, so I couldn't watch that much TV," the call ground to a halt.

We all consume goods and services, but consumerism is a different animal. It creates a perpetual need and a desire to have, with a lack of permanent satisfaction when the longing is met. I didn't need speed before the phone call, but the service provider attempted to create that need.

Need, desire, and the illusion of satisfaction are potent ingredients, especially if you fold in some entitlement.

As I watch commercials that tell me I not only need but *deserve* a new house, loan, credit card, or adventure, I find myself quietly agreeing. No longer thankful for my accommodation, financial situation, or vacation plans, I need more. Desire kicks in, and I long for the new thing that supposedly brings fulfillment.

What's missing? Gratefulness. Coveting and craving lead to consuming and a subtle discontentment. When I'm thankful for what I have, I'm content and not always aspiring for more.

I'm grateful for my internet speed.

Pause and Reflect

If we resist the grasp of consumerism, we experience gratitude for what we already possess.

Rating Other Generations

AS A BABY BOOMER, I've participated in many conversations where the younger generations are described with broad, sweeping generalizations. They aren't grateful. Don't work long and hard. Pay too much attention to work-life balance. Never stick to one thing. Expect handouts. Aren't loyal to institutions. Are short on commitment. And the biggest indictment of all? They're entitled.

That's quite a damning description—*entitled*. It means you believe you deserve special privileges and treatment. Sounds egocentric, even arrogant.

"When I grew up," says my nostalgic peer, with that smug baby-boomer attitude, "we were taught to work long and hard. Many of us showed our commitment by staying in the same company for decades. We were faithful and committed. We stuck at things.

"Unwavering support for your synagogue, mosque, or church, along with the local sports team and your preferred political party, was the way to be."

While expressing all these spectacular virtues, we'd prefer

not to mention that growing up, we were also reading books and attending workshops on burnout, work-life balance, stress reduction, exercise, time management, and proper eating. As we got older, cardiovascular challenges increased, our collective weight grew, and the time it took to eat breakfast was elongated because of all the medication we had to take.

We'd also prefer not to talk about all the carrots we were promised. If we worked hard at school, we'd get good grades, leading to desirable employment, which would give us a sustainable income and set us up nicely for retirement. Some of the carrots worked for some of the people some of the time. But sadly, many of us have entered our later years with disappointment and disillusionment.

Boomers have been recipients of the cultural message about earning and deserving. "You worked hard," we were told, "so you've earned—and deserve—all the privileges that have come your way."

So-called successful boomers need to disentangle the relationship between earning and deserving and be more honest with ourselves about the privileges we've experienced. Awareness of these privileges will move us toward more frequent thank-yous and away from an obsession with rating other generations.

Pause and Reflect

If we are immune to the reality that we lack gratitude, we may characterize a younger generation as entitled.

Othering Others

I'VE EXPERIENCED AND OBSERVED a lot of othering.

Being born a Protestant, not a Roman Catholic, in the Republic of Ireland, I remember learning that all of life could be understood through religious heritage.

As a child in the 1950s, I remember being told to close the car windows because there were people of color at the intersection.

I know a lot of people who see nonheterosexual people as less-than because they "aren't like" themselves.

As a middle-class person, it is easy for me to see those with less money as less valuable.

When Protestants other Catholics, white people other black people, straight people other nonstraight people, and middle-class people other less financially secure people, they see individuals and groups as different from them. More importantly, they are being read through one lens, whether religious affiliation, skin color, sexual preference, or financial success.

Typically that lens is pointed in a downward direction. I'm above you; you're below me. My people aren't your people, and your people aren't my people. By othering you, we will have social distancing of a particular kind.

I was part of a community where the board chair, who was gay and married to his husband, was doing an incredible amount of work. Serving above and beyond the call of duty, he significantly assisted many of us, including me.

In the world of othering, his sexual orientation would make him different from me, a heterosexual male. It could also lead me to deny his influence on myself and others. In the process, I wouldn't need to express gratitude.

When I sent him a personal letter to express my thanks for all that he had done on our behalf, I was not merely focusing on his excellent work, which was undeniable. I acknowledged his influence on me, and more importantly, I wasn't treating him as other than me.

Each culture needs to identify who is being othered and why. Who is being depersonalized and made distant? Who do we assume doesn't deserve our thanks? Othering would lessen if we increased the frequency of gratitude and decreased our social distance.

Pause and Reflect

If we recognize that no one is beneath us, we will acknowledge others' positive impact on us through expressing gratitude.

Thanking Children

THE FIRST SIXTY YEARS of parenting are the most challenging.

Rearing a child starts (after nine months of preparation) with an experience called labor. After excruciating and unspeakable pain for the aspiring mother, we start getting used to this new person who does not speak to us. Then all the markers of development become our preoccupation. Sitting, crawling, talking, toilet training, walking, running, playing. Will they do them all at the right time?

Then they move into school, with new standards for maturity. Behavior in school, in the playground, in the home. Ability to play with others. Developing friends. Treating people well. Doing homework. Believing the right things. The parental burden is immense.

High school. Anxieties about friends, influences, mental health, sexuality, drugs of various sorts. Followed by the move out of the teenage years into adulthood, where concerns continue. New criteria for belief and behavior envelop us as parents, and we hope they launch well and live the rest of their lives as happy and healthy adults.

It's exhausting. We give, tutor, guide, mentor, discipline,

sacrifice, coach, and often expect gratitude. Our children become our project, and we hope that they'll be thankful for all we've done for them.

But what if that approach got turned on its head? What if we didn't see our children as recipients of our remarkable influence toward specific behavior and belief? What if we instead emphasized belonging, where our effect on each other was valued? Recognized that their influence on us deserves our gratitude?

My daughter has taught me a lot. And although I appreciate that she expresses gratitude to Bev and me for who we are and what we do for her, I'm becoming more aware of my need to express gratitude to her for who she is and what she's done for me. My long-standing obsession with her having the correct beliefs and engaging in appropriate behavior is shifting as I learn that the third *b*—belonging—matters.

In the sphere of belonging, parenting is not solely a top-down relationship where I, the parent, push and prod to produce belief and behavior in my child, so she expresses gratitude to me. It's also recognizing that who she is and what she does deserve my gratitude. I wonder if the quality of our relationship with our children would increase if gratitude started moving in a different direction.

Pause and Reflect

If parents believe gratitude should be given to their children, they can expect growth in that relationship.

Living in the Past

RECENTLY WE HAD A COUPLE over for dinner whom we hadn't seen in forty years. There were lots of shared memories and funny stories, along with the usual organ recital, as we talked about which parts of our body aren't functioning as well as they did in the past.

In the course of the conversation, the husband shared that something I'd said to him four decades ago had had a profound effect on his life's direction, and he wanted to express his gratitude. My memory of what I said was sketchy at best, but he acknowledged the depth of his gratitude.

It made me think of similar situations. My colleague from the 1980s still thanks me for calling the police and having her hospitalized the night she was in the act of taking her own life. The woman involved in a complicated affair with a prominent leader over thirty years ago still emails to thank me for the helpful direction I provided at that time. The letter I received from a man expressing his appreciation for my part in his life when he was a confused and troubled teen still encourages me.

These experiences of being thanked for my contributions to others' lives have made me realize that I'm not as good at this form of gratitude. It's easy to get on with your life, forgetting those who have influenced you positively and failing to thank them again.

Recalling the past and expressing gratitude in the present isn't merely a repetition of what's already been said. An act worthy of thanks in the past takes on a whole new perspective when looked at across a distance of time.

As I look back over almost seven decades of life, I remember that some people started me on a journey in my twenties. I was thankful then, but now that the tapestry of my life has been woven more fully, I see how their input has had much more significance than I realized initially. I wonder if I need to spend more time looking back.

Pause and Reflect

If we revisit someone's impact on us from the past, our gratitude will deepen.

Deepening Mutuality

IT WAS ONE OF MY FIRST STAFF MEETINGS in a new organization. We went through the agenda, and when we got to the "any other business" section, one staff member declared, "I think that we should formally thank the directors for the annual salary increase they just approved." I was impressed. Proposing a motion of gratitude seemed appropriate. Who isn't thankful for more money?

But my enthusiasm was squashed quickly when another staff member said, "Why would we thank the directors for an increase when that's their responsibility?" She went on to say, "Looking after the financial well-being of staff is what they should be doing. I'm not sure why we need to thank them."

In this case, salary increases from the directors were funneled through a particular paradigm. From a perspective tinged with entitlement, directors were seen as responsible for feeding the sense of what was deserved and expected. *We deserve more money; therefore, we expect it. You have the responsibility to make those decisions, so why would we thank you?*

One of the by-products of this kind of thinking is that

the relationship with the other isn't enhanced. You are "out there" in directors' meetings, discussing budgets, allocating revenues while watching expenses. We "in here" don't see you do this, nor do we understand the nature of your deliberations. You are functionaries, doing tasks, making decisions. We are simply the beneficiaries.

Gratitude has the potential to shift the functionary–beneficiary relationship to make it more relational. What if the directors' chair had met with the staff and put a human face to the salary increase? What if they described the process that led to the decision and the directors' appreciation for the employees' work? What if the staff had sent a representative to the following directors' meeting expressing gratitude for the rise in salaries and the work that led to such a decision?

If organizations learned the power of mutual gratitude and moved away from the language of "the staff" and "the directors," there would be a more profound sense of connection.

Pause and Reflect

If we thank those who have a responsibility to us, we create an opportunity to deepen our relationship with them.

Acknowledging Impact

FOLLOWING THE HEART ATTACK, I was assigned to a cardio-rehab program. Overseen by a cardiac nurse and a fitness trainer, we listened to a cardiac-science lecture and had a strenuous guided workout every week for a year.

Polly, the nurse, had worked on cardiac units for years and had proficiency in every aspect of heart malfunction. She was a fund of information, and I felt like I could have earned a degree in heart issues just spending time with her.

Yves, the trainer, knew all about the body, cardiovascular medicine, and names for various parts of my body unknown to me. He knew when to push, when to hold back, and when to ask how you were really doing.

They were there to serve those experiencing heart issues, and it was their job to do so. I was entitled to receive what they were giving as one of the program's patients who had paid for the service. If that was the end of the story, gratitude wasn't necessary.

Toward the end of the program, I wrote a letter to the cardiologist who ran the unit, telling him about my experience with Polly and Yves. I tried to emphasize the personal variables they brought to their work and pointed out how their service seemed more than just that. They seemed to care for all of us genuinely.

A few weeks later, I was quite taken aback when Polly and Yves told me how my letter had affected them. They were so appreciative and grateful and felt acknowledged in ways that I would never have imagined. As professionals in the health-care industry who get paid for what they do, they received another window into their work through my letter.

Beyond merely providing a service, they were acknowledged for who they were by my expression of how they'd influenced me.

Pause and Reflect

If we take the time to acknowledge those who serve us, they'll find more meaning in their service.

Grateful Complementarity

AFTER FOUR YEARS OF DATING and nearly forty-five years of marriage, I find it hard to believe I've been with Bev for almost fifty years. What a patient woman.

We've had many highlights and low points during those years, lots of counseling both individually and as a couple, and we're very aware of our differences. I'm the organizer. She's more of a free spirit. I like early to bed. She's a night-hawk. I love variety. She's content with sameness. I'm more hare. She's more tortoise. I lean clean. She leans messy. I reflect on tomorrow. She lives for today. I'm active. She meditates.

Early in our relationship, my grid for these differences was straightforward: *You're wrong, and I'm right.* Marriage became a manipulative process where I, the right one, corrected her, the wrong one.

It was an impressive display of one-upmanship. An organized, early-to-bed, into-variety hare who loves clean, thinks about tomorrow, and is active far surpasses a tortoise who lives for today, meditates, loves sameness, leans messy, and is a free-spirited nighthawk.

Gratitude? Not a chance. Her qualities were a problem that needed fixing.

Later in the relationship, I moved from manipulation to tolerance. I no longer went after her for pathological and unproductive qualities but held my breath and exhibited patience at least externally while carrying minimal gratitude for who she was.

Over time, I've realized that my spouse's qualities, particularly those different from mine, are worthy of gratitude, not disdain. Bev's characteristics contribute in complementary ways to my own and, in some cases, offset the weaknesses latent in my strengths.

The tortoise has a lot to contribute to the hare. A free spirit who lives for today can provide a counterbalance to the organized one living for tomorrow.

If we don't acknowledge this reality in our long-term relationships, we position the other as unappreciated and unacknowledged. Expressing gratitude in our long-term relationships might move us out of manipulation, through tolerance, and beyond.

Pause and Reflect

If we are grateful for complementary qualities in our long-term relationships, others will feel acknowledged and appreciated.

Part Two

I'm Sorry

NINETEENTH-CENTURY POET Emily Dickinson captures the essence of remorse in simple and yet profound language:

Remorse is memory awake.[1]

To experience remorse, then, is to come awake to our memories, to understand them in a different light.

We've said or done something that's affected another person negatively. Instead of moving on, in a spirit of denial or avoidance, the incident arises in our mind. Memory awakens and provides an invitation. Will we engage in the process of self-examination with appropriate remorse and address the wrongdoing? Or will we forget and allow a relational breach to continue, unsolved and unaddressed?

Referencing these incidents where we've wounded someone else, Dickinson calls them "a presence of departed acts at window and at door." We may be in our safe house, oblivious to what we've done to others, but the person we've hurt gazes through the window, wondering whether we'll remember. At the door waits another party hoping that we'll recall the incident and invite them in for resolution. But normally, if remorse isn't embraced, memory doesn't kick in, and the departed acts remain in the past.

Within the sheltered home, multilayered curtains are put up on the windows, and dead bolt locks are screwed to the door. Departed acts aren't seen or understood. Maybe what occurred has been forgotten. Possibly self-righteousness has taken over, with no sense of personal responsibility. Perhaps a posture of victimization has been embraced, where the other is blamed. You're at fault; I'm not.

However, the experience of remorse is different. The word, from the Latin *remorsum*, means biting back or biting in return. We've brought something negative into someone else's life, and our "bite" has inflicted pain. Now we come to grips with what we did, we are "bit" in return, and we experience our own ache. In the process, we are provided with an opportunity to say "I'm sorry."

In contrast, a blame-shifting pandemic has infiltrated contemporary culture. Sophisticated explanations replace responsibility for the pain inflicted on others. Perpetrators become victims, and harm-doers are looking for sympathy. "It's not my fault" is both a verbal expression and an attitudinal posture, and the simple words "I'm sorry" are notably absent from our discourse. Individuals, leaders, organizations, systems, and countries seem to regard the articulation of remorse as a symbol of weakness.

As a Christian, I don't want to act like I'm better than everyone else and any wrong that happens in my life can be traced to others. I don't want to be known as someone who can't say "I'm sorry" but lives in victimized blame shifting, where all my problems are attributed to others.

Why?

Christians of all stripes understand that we are made of strength and weakness. Fallen image-bearers, theologians call us. Created in the image of God, with all the dignity and value that beginning provides every person on the planet. Like everyone else, many of us are great employees, parents, partners, citizens, and friends, reflecting that we are bearing God's image to some degree. That is cause for celebration— even worship of God.

But we also have a strong tendency to mess up, struggle, sin, hurt others, as the designation "fallen" indicates. We're like everyone else. Many of us blow it at work, in the home, out in the community, and with those we love. Our fallenness shows up in all sorts of ways. That's cause for "I'm sorry"—even remorse.

Those of us who are Christians need not just a recollection of the wrongs we've done to others but an awakened memory to the entire Christian story and the centrality of Jesus. Memory loss in both areas will make it more likely that we'll ignore the profound meaning of the simple phrase "I'm sorry."

In the following twenty stories on remorse, you'll read about various spheres of life and the way I, and others, have navigated remorse in a culture preoccupied with victimization.

Reading about remorse is challenging because it isn't an optimistic and happy subject, at least not on the surface. Remembering mistakes, errors, and even sins isn't a pleasant experience. It's a bite-back experience. More comfortable, by far, to close the curtains and bolt the door rather than face the fact we may have hurt others and need to move down roads of remorse, resolution, and restitution.

Again, read slowly. Free-associate to your own stories. Are there relationships or spheres where you need to let the light in and allow the breezes to blow? As you reflect on the wisdom statements, ask yourself: *What is the connection between behavior and consequence for me?* As you think about moving ahead, could you reauthor your story to be wiser and more virtuous?

As you read, imagine what the world would be like if we said "I'm sorry" as an expression of remorse in a culture that says "It's not my fault" as an expression of victimization.

I'm Sorry, But . . .

ONE OF THE WORST PHRASES IN THE WORLD is "I'm sorry, but . . ."

Most of us have perfected this approach to relationships. You've done or said something inappropriate. At least according to someone else. Deep down, you have no feeling of remorse, repentance, or anything else that smacks of guilt and regret. You're pretty ticked off that you've been told you were out of line.

You know that the words "I'm sorry" require a distinct look on the face, tone in the voice, and slant of the forehead, so you do the dress rehearsal in your head and prepare yourself to express the shortest "I'm sorry" ever. Then you drop your "but . . ." and present your case with eloquence. And arrogance.

I've perfected this skill in marriage.

Because I know it's important to apologize to Bev, I try to practice that habit. I am, after all, writing a book on the subject. Sadly, I recognize that sometimes "I'm sorry" is simply the launchpad for what my wife calls my "lawyer mode."

It's a three-step formula. First, utter the words "I'm sorry" with the right look on your face, but try to keep those words to less than three seconds. Second, insert a "but . . ." This is key because it allows you to pivot away from what you've done. Again, it's best to say this quickly so you can get to the third component, which is always characterized by the same trajectory. Completely ignore your behavior and focus exclusively on what she did.

If the lawyer mode—compelling arguments expressed rapidly, with little opportunity for interruption—is effective, I can convince Bev that there's no need for me to apologize. The goal is that she'll see the error of her ways, begin to realize that I'm in the right, and apologize for what she's done, including the terrible mistake of telling me I did something wrong.

With such a precise formula, I'm amazed at how infrequently it helps our marriage.

Quality apologies focus on our behavior. Defective expressions focus on what others did. And almost always, they include a big "but . . ."

Pause and Reflect

If we're concerned with our negative impact on others, our apologies won't contain a qualifier.

Both Wrong

MANY OF THE PROBLEMATIC relational situations I've encoun-
tered over the years have the unifying thread of an accom-
panying belief and behavior. The belief is that the other
person is wrong and needs to understand that reality. The
resultant behavior is a demanding expression of the belief
where the other is told, in no uncertain terms, that the
relationship will only change if they admit they're wrong.
Rarely, if ever, does this work.

I remember the intensity of one husband who was physi-
cally and verbally abusing his wife because she pushed a
grocery cart down the processed-food aisles when he'd told
her not to. She was wrong and needed to acknowledge that.
Noticeable by its absence was any sense of wrongdoing on
his part for berating his wife over the selection of grocery
aisles.

Family members who haven't spoken for decades usually
present a similar story. She's wrong, and until she realizes
that, nothing will change. Noticeable by its absence is any
sense that a conversation is necessary. There's no mutuality,

no desire to understand what role both people played in the relational fracture when that interaction occurs.

Political discourse, both national and international, demonstrates the same tendency. If the other is so wrong, why would we ever say we're sorry? If we're always right, why would there be any need to experience remorse?

The workplace is no different. Bosses and administrators make mistakes and engage in wrongdoing that warrants an apology to employees. There are seasons when the staff hold inappropriate attitudes toward their superiors, and an expression of "I'm sorry" would not only be appropriate but would positively influence the workplace culture. But the sad reality is that many workplaces lack a culture of mutual responsibility.

Many marriages, families, countries, and workplaces have lingering woundedness because an either-or perspective is brought to remorse. I wonder what would happen if we realized that it isn't sufficient to designate one party as wrong or right and instead embraced our shared responsibility to say "I'm sorry."

Pause and Reflect

If we are committed to the mutuality of relationships, we know that both parties likely need to embrace the importance of remorse.

Providing Accuracy

HAVE YOU NOTICED that sometimes when people say they're sorry, you wonder if they're sorry for the right thing?

An employee had worked in our department for a long time, and she seemed to be with us, missionally and relationally. But I'd get feedback that she was criticizing the company's direction and various employees.

When this approach moved from isolated incidents to a more regular pattern, I told her that I wanted to talk with her about these criticisms.

She arrived in my office and, before hitting the seat, exclaimed, "I'm sorry." But she then proceeded to focus on my reaction, even though I hadn't even talked about it. And she interspersed that focus with claims that I was receiving false information and people weren't telling the truth and with blanket denials that she'd said anything negative to anyone. I left the meeting not understanding the nature and purpose of the "I'm sorry." It felt like an apology that lacked genuineness and accuracy.

These days celebrities, athletes, and entertainers write

frequent "I'm sorry" press releases. A backlash ensues after a racist rant is posted online by a celebrity, and before long, they express remorse, with the usual "I didn't mean to hurt anyone." An athlete who has denied using performance-enhancing drugs for years is finally caught, which leads to "I want to apologize to my fans, my team, and my family." Reading from a prepared statement, a movie star admits to having serial affairs, saying, "I made a mistake, and I'm going to get help."

I'd love to ask the celebrity whether she thought about the racist rant and its capacity to hurt anyone before the post. To ask the athlete whether he's apologizing for drug use, the cover-up, or disappointing people. To ask the entertainer how serial affairs can be framed as a mistake.

These public displays of remorse cheapen the phrase "I'm sorry" and make it difficult to respond appropriately, especially when it's unclear what standard has been violated. You don't know if the person regrets their actions or is simply uncomfortable getting caught.

There's a rightness about the phrase "I'm sorry." But when it lacks specificity, it can seem so wrong.

Pause and Reflect

If we don't name the wrongdoing accurately, the other person may question the sincerity of the apology.

Enabling Dancers

IT HAPPENS IN THE WORKPLACE, places of worship, families, marriages, and parenting. Someone in the system makes poor choices and engages in inappropriate behavior.

Serial affairs. Abusive behavior. Uncontrolled anger. Perpetual sulking. Incessant criticism. Know-it-all attitude. Overdrinking. Violent behavior. Relentless control. Verbal tirades.

I've been stunned by how much power and control are granted to these individuals in various settings. Despite the weakness latent in their actions, they have immense strength in the system and often become the central figure around which everyone else dances.

Enablers teach those dance steps.

I've been an enabler in various systems. I know how it feels. You care about the person and want to be loyal to them, so you endure patiently with all their missteps, hoping one more chance will magically turn things around. But in the process, loyalty pushes out honesty, and you come to realize that dancing around them enables them to continue their inappropriate behavior. They continue to damage, so your enabling role, well-intentioned as it is, serves neither them nor you.

You hear and accept the frequent apologies, but you aren't sure whether extending forgiveness serves them well.

When the abusing spouse tells his wife that he wouldn't have hit her for the sixth time in the last two weeks if she'd speak to him in a kinder tone, she finds it easy to say "I'm sorry." Challenging or pushing him could result in unbearable consequences.

When the hostile and angry staff member, who has co-opted yet another meeting with highly personalized concerns, arrives at the subsequent encounter with a brief and unimpassioned "I'm sorry," it's easy to accept and believe the apology. While you know the long-standing pattern of blowup → apology → blowup, it feels too risky to halt the dance and confront the behavior head-on.

Professional dancing is magical because two people are in step and rhythm, taking cues from and doing what's best for each other. The enabling dance is clumsy. Both partners are out of step, and one of them is accorded way too much room on the floor.

Pause and Reflect

If we understand how damaging enabling can be, we know that accepting frequent apologies may not be in the best interest of those we love.

Taking Responsibility

OUR RESEARCH PROJECT'S STAFF got excited when an opportunity became available for a world-renowned expert to speak to us about the play behaviors of children with autism.

Later that week, I was confronted by my supervisor. She could hardly get the words out because she was in such a rage. She'd left the unmarked film beside our camera after the lecture. In our most recent filming session, I must have picked it up, inserted it in the camera, and recorded it over the talk. We had our usual material on the children engaging with one another—and nothing else.

I felt terrible. I apologized multiple times in the initial confrontation, knowing that saying "I'm sorry" wouldn't make the lecture reappear but might appease my boss. Not a chance. For days she expressed her anger, and it got to the point where she told me that she couldn't be in the same room with me. Our relationship was never the same.

I found that challenging and wondered if there was something I could do to make it better.

What should we take responsibility for when it comes to remorse?

I made a mistake in not double-checking whether the cassette was blank. While it wasn't intentional, it was still wrong and warranted remorse, along with an apology. I can take responsibility for all those things.

I can't take responsibility for her role in the problem by leaving an unmarked film near the camera. I wanted to. If she hadn't made her mistake, I wouldn't have made mine. But she's responsible for owning her part in the problem.

I also can't take responsibility for the fact the relationship was never the same. I owned up to the mistake, admitted I was wrong, experienced remorse, and expressed it on multiple occasions. But my supervisor is responsible for her ongoing emotional reaction to what I did.

While I know it's naive, I want to take on other peoples' responsibilities in these relational breaches. *Maybe I should do this or could do that*, I think. It's hard to remember that we're responsible *to* others but not responsible *for* them or their reactions.

Pause and Reflect

If we take responsibility for saying "I'm sorry," we need to allow others to take full responsibility for how they choose to respond.

Diverse Expressions

WHEN SOMEONE MESSES UP PUBLICLY, community members will often reflect on whether they have the proper amount of remorse.

He took their money, invested it with the promise that they'd get a high return, and now they have nothing. While he didn't do anything illegal, he had terrible judgment and now walks around like he's done nothing wrong. They did receive an apology, but they're struggling financially, and he acts like everything is great.

It's easy to dish out lines such as "He walks around like . . ." or "She acts like . . ." We presume that we've come to an accurate conclusion based on what we've seen. Often we have no idea what's going on and bring expectations of how remorse should be revealed.

When I do this with others, I usually assume that what I see is the way things are. My impeccable observation skills have allowed me to look at what appears and draw accurate conclusions about what is. Bathed in arrogance, I believe that the external always reveals the internal, and I can draw a straight line between them.

If I can't see remorse, it must not be present.

I've had to learn that remorse comes in different forms. Many experience shame that never entirely goes away, long after the event that precipitated it. Their life is tainted, and their hidden feeling is one of anguish, wondering if they'll ever recover. Their cheery demeanor in public does not reflect what they are actually feeling.

I find it troubling that I think I can accurately assess others' remorse by observing how things look. And even more disturbing that I, in contrast, want others to judge me solely based on how things are.

The depth of "I'm sorry" isn't easily understood through public scrutiny. It requires us to walk softly behind the masks and hear the lived experience.

Pause and Reflect

If we recognize that people express themselves in diverse ways, we will listen carefully to how each individual communicates remorse.

Remorse Brings Change

MOST OF US HAVE top-secret disgusting habits, known only to those who are close to us. One of mine is picking dead skin off my foot. Full disclosure. Sometimes I remove live skin too. My sister does it also, on her own feet, so obviously, I'm genetically victimized.

Bev and I will be sitting on the couch, and I'm subjected to a callous "What are you doing?" In marriage-speak, that means "I know what you're doing, and you know what you're doing, and I don't like it."

I try to get my hand away from my heel quickly and blurt out "What do you mean?" In marriage-speak, that means "I know you believe you caught me, but with my sleight of hand, might you have misunderstood what was happening?"

Frequently I'll say "I'm sorry," but there's no relationship between that phrase and my future foot-picking behavior.

We've all seen the religious zealot carrying a sign with the big, bold word, *Repent!* I've always wanted to interview those who pass by to ask them what they think that word means.

The Greek word for repent, *metanoia*, comes from two

smaller words: *meta*, meaning with, and *noeo*, indicating an exercise of the mind. To repent is to reassess, rethink, and reconsider with a view to change your mind. It is less focused on feeling bad about the past than on thinking about a new window into the future.

I suspect many pass him by, believing our sign-carrying friend asks people to feel bad for what they've been doing. If that's the case, the sign might be better off having the phrase "Feel remorse!" in a substantial font. But his sign points to a changing of mind, being transformed, having a conversion. It implies leaving an old road and cleaving to a new one.

When Bev does her marriage-speak about my disgusting habit and I provide my token apology, I feel remorse. But before long, my feet will get that highly personalized treatment again. If the religious zealot comes into the room with his repent sign and I follow it literally, however, foot-picking will end. Bev will be pleased.

Pause and Reflect

If our experience of remorse includes a commitment to change, it's much more likely our inappropriate behaviors will cease.

Making Amends

MY FRIEND DECIDES to visit the restroom in the middle of the meal. He pulls his chair out while simultaneously moving his body backward and upward, and the edge of the tablecloth catches on his belt buckle. In that moment frozen in time, the cloth lurches, my friend gasps, glasses begin their slow decline toward the table surface, various liquids start to overflow in multiple directions, carrots make their way onto the floor, and pieces of meat plant themselves in our laps.

Two different reactions characterize spill perpetrators.

Verbalizers who do very little repeat "I'm sorry" numerous times in high-pitched, pained ways, while they stand at the table, belt still attached to the cloth. While they're feeling bad, wine continues to dribble out of the bottle onto your pants so you can feel it on your skin, garlic butter still drizzles onto the arm of your sweater from the upended container, and water drips out of the pitcher onto your shoes.

Perpetrators who understand remorse don't just express their apologies. They dab at the mess with their napkins. They stand glasses upright. Move containers back to their vertical position. Turn up edges of the tablecloth, so no more food or drink comes off the table. Move chairs so people can escape any more spills.

No-action apologies run the risk of self-absorption. Overwhelmed with emotion for what's been done, the perpetrator pays no attention to those affected. The belt-toting spiller feels terrible but seems to have little interest in doing the remaining work so that the damage stops.

Perpetrators who see remorse as both verbal and behavioral expression look beyond their own emotional experience and ask reparation questions: *How can I make amends for what I've done? How can I lessen the pain I've inflicted?* Action follows expression, and as a result, remorse is more comprehensive.

If a simple "I'm sorry" is all we have to offer while there's a continual process of spilling wine, flowing water, and dripping garlic butter, we can be confident that the damage done will persist.

Pause and Reflect

If my apology focuses on how others are impacted, it'll include further steps to lessen the pain I've caused.

Reasons and Excuses

ALTHOUGH I'M NOT OFTEN pulled over by the police for speeding, I do have a well-rehearsed line: "I'm sorry, but I was in a hurry."

I've never worked in law enforcement, but I suspect various versions of that phrase have been offered from multiple car windows as the officer pulls out her device to print the ticket. It's stating the obvious. If you were going fast, you were obviously in a hurry. To use that awful, contemporary phrase—*it is what it is.*

What's disturbed me most when I've used this explanation for my behavior is that the officer doesn't stop issuing the ticket and exclaim, "Oh—alright, then. My mistake. Have a good day." Somehow my reason isn't easily translated into an excuse. Even though I can justify my behavior and even defend it, I still have to bear the consequences for speeding. In other words, having a rationalization for doing something wrong doesn't make it right.

A speeding trick that I haven't employed to date is questioning whether the radar gun was accurate. Speeding?

I wasn't speeding. I looked at my speedometer when you flagged me down, and I was driving under the speed limit. Like the justification of being in a hurry, the defense of "I'm not wrong, but you are" won't result in the avoidance of a ticket, although it may be worth a try.

In your relational context, have you noticed that some people employ these strategies when they've done something wrong in general or to you in particular?

You confront them on their behavior, which you or others deem inappropriate. Rather than accepting responsibility for their behavior and the pain caused, they sidestep an apology. You receive a defensive justification and come away with the sense that they think *you* should be apologizing to *them*.

It's emotional whiplash when the perpetrator of wrong, who should be expressing their remorse for what they've done, turns the situation around and becomes the victim requiring an apology. Perpetrators who become victims still deserve the ticket.

Pause and Reflect

If we grasp the true nature of apology, we'll be less likely to explain, justify, and defend.

High-Quality Remorse

YOU CONFUSE TWO DAYS in your calendar and miss a coffee date with an acquaintance. The next day you send a text: "My bad for yesterday. Sorry about that."

You're at a work party, and a colleague points out one of your weaknesses in front of senior managers. The next day she sends a text: "My bad for last night. Sorry about that."

As he walks out the door to work, your roommate loudly swears at you because of something you said. An hour later, you get a text: "My bad for swearing. Sorry about that."

All three texts express remorse through the phrases "My bad" and "I'm sorry." And yet, how can the same language serve scenarios as divergent as forgetting a coffee date and swearing at your roommate? Does "My bad" account for an act of professional humiliation?

Self-understanding, a knowledge of the other, and a clear sense of the action's severity compose high-quality remorse.

Missing a meeting may not mean much to the person with the complicated calendar, but it might be significant for the person who was stood up. A text will be sufficient in certain circumstances, but not everyone experiences being stood up in the same way.

Publicly shaming a colleague in front of superiors raises questions about intent. Why would someone do that to a fellow worker? But it also speaks to impact. What is it like to experience that level of public exposure? A text is never appropriate in those circumstances unless it's a meeting request for more dialogue.

Authentic, high-quality remorse begins with personal acknowledgment and attentiveness to the seriousness of the situation. It's an act of paying attention, committing to a different way forward. "I take full responsibility" opens the door to reconciliation and a path to a better future. "It's all my fault" invites a dialogue about the nature of the restoration. Loudly swearing roommates will find that strategy more helpful than brief texts.

Colloquial phrases like "My bad" or "Sorry about that" tend to be door-closers and run the risk of minimizing the inappropriate behavior and dismissing the other's concerns. Simply saying "I'm sorry" could end up being deeply wrong.

Pause and Reflect

If we express remorse in a way that fits the action, we create a context for quality reconciliation.

Openness to Remorse

A FEW YEARS AGO, my wife and I took a historical tour through the streets of Belfast. The community has moved toward peace and extreme violence has ceased, but consequences of the tension between Catholics and Protestants remain.

Certain taxi companies will transport Catholics to the downtown core, but not Protestants. Neighborhoods are segregated according to religious expression. Our guide talked about the fracture in his family because he'd married someone from the other side.

The saddest part of the tour was hearing how the children believed that they were right and the other side was wrong. They were unaware of all the history, but they learned a valuable lesson early on. Since *we* are correct, we can blame *them* for being wrong. No apology is needed. When that mindset is planted, fertilized, and watered in childhood, it bears fruit across the generations.

Many people are raised to believe that individuals are to be understood based solely on their link with a particular group. African Americans. Indigenous peoples. Democrats. Republicans. Liberals. Conservatives. Atheists. Christians. Jews. Straight people. Gay people. Immigrants. Migrants.

The fruit of this style of child-rearing is that individuals aren't valued for who they are but caricatured negatively based on their group affiliation. Their core is less vital than their communal connection. If we have a problem with their collective, we assume all the individuals within it are wrong. Because we're right, there's no need to be open to remorse. No need to be willing to say "I'm sorry."

In the suburbs of Belfast, religious factions are on full display with peace walls. Up to twenty-five feet in height and ranging in length from two hundred yards to three miles, these structures were implemented to prevent violence. The Catholic nationalists who understand themselves as Irish see one side of the wall, while the Protestants who align with Britain see the other side.

Ironically, the adjective *peace* is in front of the noun *wall*. Real peace has no barrier. When the wall's destruction does occur, it won't be traced to heavy machinery but softened hearts.

Pause and Reflect

If we value each individual's dignity rather than negatively caricature their group affiliation, we'll be free to express remorse.

Revisiting Our Narrative

IT WAS ONE OF THOSE MEETINGS that are hard to forget. Two members of our community wanted to meet with the leadership team to express their concerns. If you've ever had a leadership role, you know that about 89 percent of the time, "express concerns" means you'll be criticized.

It was a lengthy diatribe of accusations that all fit a tightly defined narrative. We were inadequate leaders who made inappropriate decisions, miscommunicated, and most damning of all, this was a persistent pattern that had gone on for some time. Under our boss's careful instruction, we absorbed the pain, took the hit, and didn't react. He told us that there might come a time when they'd be sorry for what they said in the meeting.

These two individuals had a story in their heads about the leadership of that organization. A decision we'd recently made fit the narrative entirely, or so they thought. They now had another example of how poorly we were guiding the community.

Internal narratives are like that. They help us interpret

actions and events and then provide meaning. We often fail to realize that our narratives sometimes give us a skewed view of the world. We squeeze situations to fit into our personally constructed story without realizing how much squeezing we're doing.

Many months after that event, the same two people came back to visit the leadership team, not with "concerns" but with remorse. Based on new information and greater clarity on several community dynamics, they realized they'd responded with a limited perspective. Their heartfelt apology washed over the group, and reconciliation began.

A certain kind of selflessness will aid in reconsidering, reappreciating, and reauthoring an old story. A new narrative begins to come into view as the old one is set adrift. But the time between the death of the old narrative and the birth of the new one can seem endless, especially if you've been bruised by the old one. Often the transition from death to birth is best bridged by an apology.

Pause and Reflect

If we allow new information to enter our narrative, we may discover our need to express remorse.

Self-Regulation

THOSE OF US WHO'VE LIVED through trauma know the pattern well. Experiences that remind us of times we've been abused or belittled, neglected or marginalized elicit feelings of insecurity or being unloved. We develop an almost insatiable desire for acceptance and value. But then we hit the world as it is and get triggered.

Not everyone grants us love and affirmation. Others' behavior is a subconscious reminder of early negative experiences. This feeling of revictimization produces an intense response that may be aggressive, angry, controlling, dominating, sad, and hurt. Present pain is now intertwined with past hurt.

Psychologists use the category of emotional regulation to capture this phenomenon. Those who regulate well can manage the intensity and duration of these experiences and disconnect the new encounter from the early trauma. Emotional dysregulation occurs when the present is interpreted through the lens of the past. All the feelings are brought to the table and people often find themselves in interpersonal tension that they can't resolve. Because these people often blame the person who triggered the emotion, assuming it's their fault, this further complicates the relationship.

When we're with those who don't regulate their emotions, two forms of compassion are needed—compassion for them and compassion for ourselves.

Living with trauma and triggering is exhausting, and if the person hasn't done the hard therapeutic work to deal with it, they carry an unbearable load that is hard to manage. They both desire and need our compassion.

If we're in this kind of challenging relationship, the conflict will inevitably be intense and frequently long-lasting. Our very presence in the same room may be a trigger before we say or do anything.

When anyone has been hurt or mistreated, it's right and proper to apologize. "I'm sorry" isn't reserved for particular people. It's a gift we can give anyone.

But those who struggle with emotional regulation may not hear our apology, may indicate it was never said, may not like the way we said it, or may continually bring things up we've already addressed. In those situations, we need self-compassion and the recognition that we can't offset all the historical pain. When triggers are in play, we aren't entirely responsible for the intensity of other peoples' emotions.

Pause and Reflect

If we apologize in the best way we know how to, that doesn't always guarantee the apology will be well received.

Openhearted

AFTER FORTY-PLUS YEARS of marriage, I have come to see it as a pure distillation of each person's mix of strength and struggle.

Strength because we both bring our good sides to something much bigger than ourselves. In my marriage, our shared sense of humor and commitment to reality rather than impression is a tell-it-like-it-is sharing with each other rather than a we-are-doing-really-well-all-the-time superficiality. We also prefer candor and conflict with a desire to grow rather than have secrets, hide, and tiptoe around the truth. But out of those strengths, struggles emerge.

Bev's intuition and passion, pointed in the wrong direction, can be hurtful. My verbal strength and convictions, slanted with an improper angle, can be damaging. Our direct conflicts, while honest, can be counterproductive and infrequently even cruel.

My openness with her can trigger her foundational question, *What's wrong with me?* My core question, *Am I really loved?*, can come to the surface when she's candid with me.

In our humanness, we hurt each other.

Marriage research shows that it's challenging to predict divorce by the presence or absence of conflict. Instead, what predicts divorce is the presence or absence of respect. Minimal conflict with high disrespect is more concerning than excessive friction with high respect.

Respecting someone means according them significance and admiration. Because you know them and their essence, you've concluded they're a person of value. There's room for clashes in a mutually respectful marriage because even when pain is caused, there's an ongoing willingness to say "I'm sorry."

Willingness may be the key.

In the raw humanness of a long-standing marriage, struggle emerging from strength is inevitable. The potential for hurting the other is high. And strangely, the stakes get higher as you get older. More time can lead to increased conflict and produce resentment and bitterness, even cynicism. Nothing is more painful to watch than an older married couple who have nurtured years of other-inflicted pain hold it against one another in spirit and facial expression.

Being openhanded and openhearted with apologies supplies the soothing oil that'll ease the abrasion of relational tension. Willingness to apologize doesn't remove the conflict but provides a gentle backdrop.

Pause and Reflect

If a relationship is long-standing, it requires an ongoing willingness to show respect by expressing remorse.

Forgetting the Past

BEV AND I HAVE BENEFITED from chiropractors on many occasions, but on this particular day, the outcome was different. At the beginning of the treatment, Bev was being loosened up with a gentle massage when suddenly, there was a loud crack, significant pain, and a horrified "I'm sorry." Massage usually produces soothing comfort, but this time it was one broken rib and a chiropractor in significant distress.

It was clear that the doctor felt terrible for inflicting pain; she expressed that in multiple ways. She even came to our door later that day with flowers, a card, and more apologies.

But the rib was still broken. Remorse, repentance, and apologies didn't result in the removal of pain.

I remember counseling a couple who had been hit by a drunk driver, which killed their newborn infant. The driver of the car, in a sober state, felt remorse and apologized, but that didn't bring the child back to life.

People who exert pain on others need to grapple with the reality that "I'm sorry" doesn't remove the hurt. Ribs are broken. Infants are dead. Long-term implications of both situations may be evident for many years.

But Bev and the parents have a choice of trajectory to establish going forward. The goal can't be to forget what happened or minimize its influence. As long as the hippocampus, that part of the brain responsible for memory, isn't damaged by disease or trauma, previous events will come to mind. While remembering the breaking of a rib will have minimal consequences long term, who will cease to be impacted by losing their infant daughter?

When others wrong us and express "I'm sorry," we can cultivate a posture whereby we continually hold a grievance against them, keep an indefinite record of wrongs, and always lean into vengeance and retribution.

Alternatively, we can acknowledge the event's reality because it's part of our lived experience and accept that it has influenced us. We don't review, rehearse, or repeat it so it defines us, making the offender our primary focus in the process.

Pause and Reflect

If we express our remorse, it isn't guaranteed that our wrongdoing will be forgotten or cease to affect the other person.

Act of Listening

REMORSE IS MORE ABOUT LISTENING and less about telling.

It seems counterintuitive to make such a claim because saying "I'm sorry" is about speaking. The attitude embedded in remorse, however, is probably best measured by one variable: the degree to which we've understood what the other has experienced. If I have a vague sense that I upset you and rush to apologize, I haven't given you the dignity to speak about the influence I've had on you.

Only you can express impact. I need to listen if I want to feel genuine remorse. It's one of the reasons written apologies rarely take. Only one person is talking.

I have been privileged to be in conversation with many indigenous individuals throughout my life, including Māori (the indigenous New Zealanders), Australian Aboriginals and Torres Strait Islanders, Kikuyu (an indigenous tribe in northern Kenya), and First Nations in North America.[1]

Marginalized indigenous people are beginning to find their voice. Starting to speak their truth. Willing to take the risk to confront the privileged.

They aren't merely looking for verbal expression of remorse, although that would be welcomed. Listening is desired. And not just from anyone but from those who appropriated their land, settled among them, and exerted power over them.

Recently I was in a group where a First Nations woman recounted her experience of what it was like to see her siblings taken out of their home and put into a residential school, where they learned to be "white." I was so self-conscious about my skin color that night. Teaching people to be white? Why would my ancestors pursue such an absurd goal?

At that point, my blaming of distant others receded from view, and I became aware of the subtle and not-so-subtle racism lurking in me. I wanted to say, "Stop. I hear you. We're sorry. I don't want to know any more details."

What she needed wasn't a hit-and-run apology, where my knowledge of the painful consequences was minimal. That kind of remorse was solely for my benefit. She needed to tell her story.

Saying "I'm sorry" is way easier than listening.

Pause and Reflect

If we understand remorse as an act of listening, we create opportunities for others to tell us how they experienced our actions.

No Guarantee

FLIGHT TIME FROM SYDNEY, AUSTRALIA, to my home in Vancouver, Canada, is just over fourteen hours. Four movies and a meal will get you halfway.

We've often made this trip, but unforeseen circumstances made for a challenging experience on this particular occasion. About ninety minutes after takeoff, a man had a heart attack and was resuscitated. At that point, a decision was made to turn the plane around so he could receive appropriate medical care.

When the pilot announced the circumstances, he apologized profusely and acknowledged that this would be disruptive for the rest of us. He didn't tell us that the crew would have to be changed in Sydney because the flight was now too long for the same team. By the time we landed, the patient was taken off, and the crew exchange took place, we experienced a considerable delay. And this before starting the fourteen hours all over again.

When the new pilot apologized for what had happened, I experienced strange and contradictory feelings. On the one hand, I knew the ill man's well-being needed to be addressed, but on the other, I was frustrated. The pilot was apologizing, but I wasn't getting what I wanted.

I didn't like what I saw in myself that day.

It was a mixture of expectations and victimization with a dose of individualism. I expected the usual fourteen-plus hours of travel time. That's what the airline promised. But now, I was the victim of circumstances beyond my control, and I don't like that. I was sure the ill man was a lovely person, but over three hundred of us had our lives messed up. Bev and I were most interested in our well-being. Doing what is best for others is a beautiful concept, but it has its limits, especially when you're on a plane for more than half a day.

My underlying assumption was that the apology, which addressed the consequences and disruption of the pilot's decision, should give me what I want. I've learned that there are times when hearing "I'm sorry" is no guarantee that I'll receive all of what I desire.

Pause and Reflect

If we expect apologies to give us what we want, we may be frustrated when others say they're sorry.

Communal Representative

I'VE HAD TO LEARN A LESSON that I never really understood before assuming leadership responsibilities: We can apologize on behalf of others.

When I've received negative feedback from people who had been part of the community in the past, my first instinct has been to wonder why they were raising issues with me. I wasn't present when they experienced the challenging circumstances. How could I, the new leader, address the past?

Institutions have character and personality. Attitudes are in the DNA, hidden behind the walls, and floating in the air. Often it isn't that one person does the damage but that a toxicity exists in the community's functioning. It's almost as if the individuals participate in something bigger than themselves.

Leaders not only provide direction for the organization but embody it. Embodiment means to represent, personify, and exemplify the values of the whole. To see you is to know the institution. To see the institution is to know you.

When things are going well, this linkage is powerful. We

aren't just a company that claims to care for our customers and serve them with quality. Our CEO exudes that same care and level of service when she meets with customers and all the other stakeholders. Through her, they experience the community's aspirations.

I value that leadership approach, but I didn't realize that the same principle applies when something hasn't gone well in the past.

I remember spending hours with a person who, before my arrival, had been severely abused by the organization I was leading. His story, well-documented with written material, made me sad and angry. Sad because of all that he'd gone through over many years. Angry because the way he was treated was far removed from all that we claimed to be.

My impulse was to align myself with him against *them* and stay with my sadness and anger. But then it dawned on me that *I was them*. I couldn't claim to represent the institution in the present and distance myself from everything in its past. Nor could I exemplify positive communal values and disassociate from those that were more negative.

Saying "I'm sorry for what we did" wasn't easy.

Pause and Reflect

If we represent a community, we have a responsibility to others that extends beyond our actions.

Apologizing to Children

WE WERE IN ONE of my least favorite places in the world—a mall. As we wandered up and down the aisles with their usual enticing whispers to consume, our three-year-old daughter took off.

In a previous era, my track skills were at a level where catching her would have been easy, but on this occasion, those little legs moved at such a rapid pace that she was out of sight within seconds. Our usual mall decorum was soon replaced by ear-piercing calls of "Jessica" as we rushed in and out of stores, imagining the worst and hoping for the best.

The longest three minutes of our lives ended abruptly when we realized that one of the stores housed a sizable circular skirt rack. A skirt rack large enough to accommodate a three-year-old. She hid among the skirts while we were shrieking her name.

I haven't struggled with homicidal impulses throughout my life, but at that moment, they were rising to the surface. It's a strange brew. Fear and panic mixed thoroughly with overwhelming relief, all folded together with shock, anger, and rage, with a heavy dose of stunned disbelief. Not only did you run away, but you hid, and not only did you hide, but you heard Mommy and Daddy's pleading cries, and you stayed in the skirt rack? What were you thinking?

Parents who've experienced that particular brew know the nature of the next frame in the video. It wasn't pretty as she endured being a captive audience to me giving full vent to my contradictory emotions.

It ended the way it needed to end. She was wrong for doing what she did and needed to express her remorse. But I was wrong in my response to what she did. Unbridled rage and shame-filled name-calling are neither respectful nor a punishment that is commensurate with the crime.

"I'm sorry" is something we should expect from our children. Not infrequently, we ought to give it to them.

Pause and Reflect

If we understand that parents aren't always right, we'll embrace opportunities to apologize to our children.

Priority of Dialogue

MANY PEOPLE HAVE BEEN RECIPIENTS of abuse from a family member over a lengthy period. It's one thing to experience a single incident of relational fracture with a friend, but quite another to be in anguish over painful experiences within the family. From a young age, we expect those close to us to communicate love and care, so it's emotionally jarring when the opposite occurs.

Counseling for abuse usually focuses on a fourfold process of naming the experience, identifying emotions, moving toward healing, and meeting with the problematic family member. While engaging with the abuser is not always possible, the ideal is to move from intrapersonal resolution to interpersonal healing. Both parties can hear and be heard in the presence of a third party who facilitates the interaction and creates a safe environment.

If the meeting with the family member occurs, one of three outcomes is typical. In some cases, there's a genuine expression of remorse combined with healthy dialogue and shared understanding. At other times there's denial, justification, or defensiveness with little healing. The most emotionally confusing situation is when there's an "I'm sorry" with minimal dialogue or understanding of the nature of the damage.

I've witnessed the pain of many people coming back from these interactions, bewildered by the inequity. She did this to me over all these years, and all she could say is "I'm sorry"? He's acted inappropriately almost our entire relationship, and he thinks saying "I'm sorry" will get rid of the hurt?

High-quality remorse isn't a single brief apology for actions and attitudes in the past. It isn't a way to bring immediate closure to pain experienced over many years. Instead, it's a door opener, where there's a desire to listen and understand. It is the commencement of a new way of being, not just the abrupt end of something negative.

When you find out you've hurt someone over a long time, everything in you wants to use "I'm sorry" to bring the conversation to an end. But having a genuine, empathic interest in the influence we've had on others is remorse of a different kind.

Pause and Reflect

If we've created long-standing pain for others, our remorse needs to be paired with dialogue and increased understanding.

Part Three

Tell Me More

IN HER HISTORICAL NARRATIVE on Joseph, Jacob's deserted son, American writer Madeleine L'Engle carefully unpacked the customs and culture around this crucial figure in Jewish history. She did this for a specific reason: We need to consider the full contours of a story to understand the *why* behind the *what*. She saw this as more than just a matter of history; it's a central problem of contemporary culture:

> Because we fail to listen to each other's stories, we are becoming a fragmented human race.[1]

L'Engle rightly described our current circumstances. Fragmented. Broken down into separate parts and disengaged segments. We lack connection with one another when we fail to take the time to attend, be attentive, and understand.

Many of us live in apartments or townhouses, where our neighbors sleep on the other side of a poorly insulated wall, mere feet from our pillow. But our close physical proximity is out of proportion to our level of intimacy. We exchange pleasantries in the elevator, but there's a lack of mutual relationship. And not a few of us experience similar disconnection in our homes, at work, and in places of worship. And most damning of all, fragmentation births detachment, which in turn produces a lack of care.

The Old English word for care is *carian*, describing a concern for, an interest in. To care for another is to move toward them, to have an inclination, an attentiveness. When the phrase "couldn't care less" appeared in the 1800s, it helped clarify the term *care*'s essence. If I feel no positive emotion toward someone, and no desire to move in their direction, they won't receive my interest. I'll care less.

L'Engle's answer to this challenge? Listen to each other's stories.

Behind each of our facades is our personal story. Emerging from our life history, our story helps us maintain and organize our reality. It gives us meaning, an interpretation of what the world is like and how it works. As various events occur, we fit them into our story, and when they don't correspond to our inner narrative, we experience a disconnect. Our story is the core of who we are, interwoven with where we've been, where we are, and where we're going. To know me is to know my story. To only see my behavior and hear my words is to miss my story.

Preoccupation with our own story leads us to not care about the stories of others. When my story matters most, I have been lured in by the individualism of the culture. Life revolves around me. My capacity to listen to others is limited, and I rarely say "Tell me more."

Listening to other people's stories is hard work. It requires attentiveness and engagement to move from the shallow end out into deeper water. Stories are complicated and messy, circular and angled, and offer an invitation to care and not cure, be present and not solve. And they take time to tell. There are no shortcuts for listening to stories. While various cyberspace-communication modes can relay information, listening to stories requires a thoughtfulness that is best expressed face-to-face, over time, with respectful curiosity. Saying "Tell me more" involves sacrifice. Sacrifice for the other.

Not listening to each other's stories may be one of the essential elements missing in contemporary culture. As L'Engle argued, it may also give us a glimpse into why there's so much fragmentation.

As a Christian, I want to be known as someone who listens to the stories of others. But I know the stereotype. Christians talk and tell, preach and proselytize. We are known as people who want to influence, not attend. Communicating our story is a much higher value than engaging others' stories.

When I read about Jesus, I'm struck by how different he was from many Christians (an odd sentence, I know). When he interacted with people, he listened.[2] So much of his teaching came out of the subtleties and nuances embedded in others' stories.[3] As he attended to what they were saying, he'd build off a word, a turn of phrase, a throwaway comment, and pull their story together into his own.[4]

While Jesus lived by conviction and principle, you never get the sense that this was to exclude others and their experiences. As he listened, he said things that could only come from the perspective of really hearing the other. Why would he tell a respectable religious man he needed to be born again but discuss worship with an immoral outcast woman? Wouldn't you think a woman caught in the act of adultery would get a rougher ride from Jesus than the men who exposed her? These paradoxes are only explainable through understanding his ability to listen to others' stories.

And if I broaden beyond Jesus to the rest of the Christian Scriptures, so much of it is story. Stories about God's work in the world. Experiences of humans tainted by brokenness relayed on the sacred page—lives of saints, sinners, and skeptics, all woven together as part of a bigger story. You could argue that a proper reading of the Bible requires us to listen well to others' stories.

The following twenty vignettes provide another opportunity to reflect on your own story. Are you a person who expresses care by communicating an inner spirit and a verbal expression of "Tell me more"? Has the individualism of the culture made you more interested in your own story? Thoughtful and slow reading of these stories will bring encouragement and enhance your ability to care. Most importantly, it will help change the world.

As you read, imagine what the world would be like if we said "Tell me more" as an expression of care in a culture that says "My story matters most" as an expression of individualism.

Talking Too Much

ISN'T IT FASCINATING to be in a room, online, on the phone, or in a car with an overtalker? Maybe *fascinating* isn't the right word, but it's fun to observe.

They talk and talk and talk and talk. I'm always intrigued by the combination—they're seemingly able to inhale, exhale, and speak at the same time. It's quite a feat to be able to do all three simultaneously. I've found myself wondering how this is even possible from a physiological standpoint.

As the listener, you have to strategize your entry. You wait for a larger-than-usual inhale or exhale in the hopes that this will be your chance. If you can just interrupt the flow, you might have a chance of getting a word in. If you do get a foot in the door, I often find one of two things happens.

Typically, the speed ramps up, their flow of words is undiminished, you're interrupted, and the door gets closed. Sometimes they do stop, but then it's not long before you understand, again, what the phrase "drinking from a fire hose" really means.

If you pay money, buy a ticket, and become part of the

audience in a public lecture, you expect the person at the front to keep talking, influencing, sharing, and persuading. You paid your money so they could speak, and you could listen, so the lack of mutuality isn't off-putting. But when you want to tell someone from the neighborhood, family, church, synagogue, or mosque that you didn't buy a ticket and aren't sitting on a plush chair as a member of the audience enjoying their monologue, something is wrong.

Listening is a lost art.

Listening isn't easy: It requires self-control, genuine interest, curiosity, and valuing others more than ourselves. Like dancing, it requires a rhythm where the blend of telling and hearing is seamless and easy. It isn't that one person unloads while the other is in a hypnotic trance, followed by a reversal of roles. It's a reciprocal give-and-take where people share and absorb in a natural, unchoreographed way, offering "Tell me more" and cherishing each other's stories. Overtalking finds no partner in that kind of dance.

Pause and Reflect

If we listen more and speak less, the stories of others become relevant.

Speaking with Others

IT WAS PROBABLY one of the more anxiety-producing social events of my life. I was in a room with several federal politicians, including one of the party leaders. When you've only seen people on the internet or TV, you accord them stature and status, rendering you powerless and insecure.

The day before, the party leader had made bold statements on some social issues, including abortion. Press coverage had been intense, resulting in many pundits posting reactions and members of the parties lining up in predictable ways.

At one point in the event, the party leader was standing alone, and I made an impulsive decision to cross the room and initiate a conversation. My motivation came from a long-held frustration that most politicians seem adept at speaking *at* rather than speaking *with* others. Once they're locked into a position, they return to it over and over, and you never quite know the story behind the story.

After a few pleasantries, I took the plunge: "Tell me more about what you said at the press conference yesterday." He outlined his position and the awkwardness that he was now in a room with people who vehemently disagreed with him. Because I knew a little about his family and religious history, I took a more significant leap and asked him how his comments fit his background. That led to a fascinating discussion on how his personal story was in step with what he said in the press conference.

As our conversation ended, he expressed appreciation for it. But when he said why, I was saddened. Pointing to his critics across the room, he said, "None of them will talk with me today."

Just as politicians run the risk of speaking at, rather than speaking with, so do many others. Parents can hide behind content and not tell their stories. Religious leaders can give their sacred-text reflections but not reveal anything of themselves. Professors can offer brilliant lectures to their students but not facilitate an environment where there's a mutual sharing of stories.

We're in a time where political discourse and civil interaction are missing. Maybe we need to learn to speak with each other.

Pause and Reflect

If we speak with each other, we create a context for people to share their stories.

Communicating Impact

OVER THE LAST FORTY YEARS, I've had thousands of in-depth conversations with twenty- and thirtysomethings about their lives, aspirations, joys, and disappointments. Many of them describe their lived experience with their parents as lacking.

Even times of so-called celebration, like Thanksgiving, Christmas, birthdays, and the like, seem to fall short. Because families, like all the other structures and systems on the planet, are tainted by brokenness and failure, one might not be surprised that parents don't come through for their adult children.

When you press for explanation, the adult children often describe the experience as superficial and removed from their lives. Family interaction seems to be less focused on what's happening in me and more on what's happening around me. Conversation is more head-to-head than heart-to-heart. The impersonal trumps the personal.

This is a jarring experience for a generation growing up with a refreshing sense of vulnerability, transparency, and authenticity. If my parents are more concerned with what I have or what I'm doing and have little interest in who I am, I won't feel acknowledged.

If I don't feel known, I lose a sense of how I affect others, even my parents. How am I affecting them? Do they appreciate who I am at the core? Are they interested in what's going on in my life, beyond what they see on the surface? Are they willing to vulnerably share their inner journey, so I know their experiences? Can I do the same in reverse?

Many years ago, we started a practice in our home called "verbal bouquets." Just as a bouquet of flowers can bring joy to someone, we believe the same is true when we speak personally to others. We try to do this regularly with our daughter, as well as close family and friends, but we also ensure that all celebratory times have a component of "Tell me more." We tell the person how they've influenced us, how their various qualities have encouraged us, how who they are has brought us joy. Good food and wine are foundational to a party, but the event has much more meaning if we talk personally to others. There's buoyancy as we all walk out of the shallow water into the deep end, knowing that we mean something to each other.

Adult children would bond more closely with their parents if their times together were characterized by less superficiality and more vulnerability.

Pause and Reflect

If we celebrate people personally, we'll tell them how they impact us positively.

Breeding Self-Disclosure

I HAD A SUPERVISOR who loved reading books and going to conferences so he could master leadership skills. In one particular season, he stumbled on this unique piece of advice: If you call your employees by their first name, they'll feel like you know them, and they'll be more committed to the mission.

He'd arrive in our part of the building, greet everyone by their first name, and then hurriedly move to another area. You could tell he felt awkward, doing something that was way out of his comfort zone, but there was one unfortunate part: Many of us were called by the wrong name.

In contrast, I had a supervisor who also read books and went to conferences, but she understood leadership as an expression of who one is rather than what one does. She wasn't absorbed with the development of skills but sought to be present with those she led, inviting them into a genuine relationship for the mission's good.

When the leaders met, she'd reveal her heart and welcome others to do the same. The emphasis on our shared humanity made you feel that you weren't just a leader but a person. Not a repository of skills but someone who lived close to the ground, in copilgrimage with your colleagues. An invitational atmosphere washed over the room, with a call to know and be known. It was easy to step across that threshold.

The staff under the skill-oriented boss would laugh when he left the room, but the other supervisor had empowered and encouraged employees. The first organization's workforce found it easier to hide and avoid transparency because it wasn't modeled for them. Why would I open up to you if you don't provide an atmosphere where this is valued?

Self-disclosure breeds self-disclosure.

Leaders who want to create a safe place where people can be themselves won't produce it through demand or command. Vulnerability needs to be modeled, with all the awkwardness that this entails. Getting out from behind our masks and our concern with role and appearance isn't easy. But if we're interested in our followers telling us more, we have no choice.

Pause and Reflect

If a leader displays vulnerability, the inner experience of those they lead will be called out.

Being Opinionated

THE WORLD IS FILLED with OOEs and OOSs: Those who are opinionated on everything and those who are opinionated on something.

I've found that OOEs are stunning in the breadth of their firmly held perspectives. You can raise any subject, and it's an invitation for a rant. They pull in snippets of information, cite a podcast they listened to, relay many personal experiences, throw in passion, and express their views with conviction—and a dose of conceit.

Unlike OOEs, OOSs wait in the bushes for their subject of choice.

I was in a social event and met a certain woman for the first time. She seemed amiable, and the cadence of our conversation was relaxed—until I mentioned something about environmental concerns. She bristled, and with an angry intonation, blurted out, "I'm not a tree hugger." It turned into an OOS moment.

If you want to lure these people out of the bushes, try these lines at your next cocktail party and see who speaks up:

What do you think of Donald Trump? Is the Democratic-party platform moving to the left? Is gay marriage a civil right? Should immigration be linked with justice?

The word *opinionated* appeared in the English language in the 1600s to describe someone who held a perspective. Since some held their opinions dogmatically, the word gradually took on a more pejorative meaning.

The difference between having an opinion and being opinionated revolves around the experience of the listener.

I love being in a room with people who have opinions. Having thought through an issue, they share openhandedly. Without any sense, they have everything figured out. And most importantly, they invite you to do the same.

Pause and Reflect

If being opinionated is our primary mode of relating, we cut ourselves off from others.

Cultivating Friendships

IT'S HARD TO KEEP TRACK of all the contemporary acronyms, but BFF is generally understood. To use it is to speak endearingly of someone close. We are best friends forever.

My best friend in elementary school was Robbie. Danny was my BFF in high school, Janna was my person as an undergraduate, and Peter, Jim, and Rod were my BFFs as a graduate student.

Two of them have died, and I'm only in touch with one of the other four. Danny and I have seen each other twice in the last forty years, along with a few conversations online and on the phone. The final *F* has been dropped for the other five.

So, what is a friend?

Friendship sometimes emerges because of common circumstances or communities. Danny and I were in the same year in high school and played a lot of golf together. Peter and I did graduate school together, so we shared classroom and clinical experiences. I experienced unusual kinship with Jim and Rod, two of my professors.

In many ways, all these relationships were characterized

by what was happening around us. We were close, but it was circumstantial connectedness.

When I connected with any of those people in later years, we'd ask, "Where's Cherry?" "What is David doing now?" "What's Mary up to?" We'd share stories about what was happening to Cherry, the passing of Dave's brother, and the recent wedding of Mary's daughter.

Moments of nostalgia and memory are delightful as we regale each other with what was happening around and to us.

As important as "around us" and "to us" are, friendship that focuses on "in us" is the strongest. Most of us have the social skills to go to a party and talk about politics, the weather, or even our new job and our daughter's marriage.

Friendship that puts a dent in superficiality doesn't focus exclusively on "around" and "to" but is built on "in." Companions that want to know about our political views and our new job are valuable but not as impactful as those who provide an invitational "Tell me more," so we share what's in us. They are the real BFFs.

That's why Bev, Susan, Allan, Paul, Rose, Glenn, Mary, Heather Ann, James, Cathy, Steve, and others matter. We are still in relationship, through the decades, interwoven into life's fabric. You can't make old friends.

Pause and Reflect

If we're committed to the richness of what is happening in us and others, we'll cultivate long-lasting friendships.

Impression Management

IT WAS ONE OF THOSE FAMILY EVENTS that's still talked about years later.

My mother's youngest sister and her husband were visiting from Ireland. In our family system, this was an opportunity to show the success of the immigrants. The trip became a tour through the gallery of accomplishment.

For me, preparation for their visit to our house was straightforward: I put on one knee-length argyle sock, an old pair of multicolored polyester shorts, and a beat-up T-shirt with a picture of an old Ford car. The crowning touch was the shave. I removed half of my thick, bushy beard. Mid-chin to the left was clean-shaven.

I will never forget the looks on my aunt and uncle's faces when I opened the door. They were so struck by the event they still talk about it with hilarity. But I did worry that we'd need a defibrillator for my parents.

This event was my youthful, immature, passive-aggressive way of speaking against the dynamic I struggled with most in my family of origin—impression management.

My parents had been shaped by their family histories, so it was no surprise that in my upbringing, how things looked was valued more highly than how things were. I learned to look, speak, and behave the part. (A part that was mainly rooted in what others saw and what they thought.)

In our domestic play, loyalty to the family script was preferred over reading your own lines.

Impression management's major problem is that impressions mask reality. I may act the part, but when the production is over and I get into my street clothes, I leave my role behind. Person replaces role, and I need people who will push past the costume and the lighting to see the real me. People who won't be deterred by the image but want to hear my voice.

If we cultivate a way of relating to one another that isn't reflective of who we are, we aren't asking each other to tell us more. My desire to hear your story and your willingness to listen to mine move us off the stage.

To say "Tell me more" is to care about the narrative hidden behind the full beard . . . and the one partially removed.

Pause and Reflect

If we look behind the impression others create, we'll hear the stories they're living.

Beyond Evaluation

HAVE YOU EVER NOTICED how much easier it is to evaluate than to understand?

Your daughter begins telling you about a guy she met in her freshman class at university. As soon as the word *guy* is out of her mouth, your brain instantly produces a lengthy checklist. If you're a wise parent, you keep the list to yourself, make sure your face is open and welcoming, and work to ensure your breathing at least appears relaxed.

"He's older than me." Such a simple phrase, but the brain kicks into overdrive and scours the "appropriate questions" list. *Older? By how much? Is he my age? Was he married before? Does he have children? Older? Has his pension kicked in yet?*

"He seems to really like me." *What does that really mean? What does he like about you? Is he a predator? Has he ever been arrested?*

When we listen through the evaluative mode, we're a long way from the spirit of "Tell me more." We're more captivated by our internal thought processes, fears and anxieties, and our need to assign a grade. *You met someone older than you. We'll start with a B and see where we go from there. He seems to like you? We're now down to a C+.*

I've known several people who've been incarcerated. They've been arrested, charged, convicted, and penalized for their crimes. Evaluated and found wanting, they are convicted criminals. They each have their own lived experience from committing the crime through to their release, but it's significant that so many find it hard to reintegrate into society. Our need to evaluate plays a central role in that process.

One of my friends described the inability of his community to cope with him after his release. No one wanted to hear his story. Even though he'd confessed, experienced remorse, and paid the consequences for his crime, he continued to be assessed and found wanting. The evaluative preoccupation of others got in the way of their ability to hear what he went through during incarceration. His communal life after release became a prison of another sort.

Pause and Reflect

If we move beyond evaluation to understanding, we give others dignity as we affirm their humanity.

Facts and Feelings

MY WIFE AND I STARTED DATING in our early twenties. I remember all too well those early months. *What do you tell? What do you reveal? If you tell all, will she take off? If you reveal everything, will she be able to handle it?*

And then there was the other side of the relationship. *Is she telling me all of who she is? Is she hiding parts of herself, fearing that she'll be rejected? Is there anything she could reveal that will send me for the hills?*

No wonder dating is stressful. Managing secrets is hard work.

Before we got married, we made a pledge to each other. We both struggle with the reality that many individuals and families live with secrets, so we decided that our life together would be in the light. Full exposure. No hiding. No fig leaves.[1] Even if it hurts (and it did hurt at times). A commitment to reality is painful.

Part of that commitment was giving each other permission to talk about historical facts and share how those facts impacted us in the present. When you're dating in your twenties and you talk about an event that occurred when you were seventeen, you have a particular emotive response and reaction. When you're married and forty-four, the historical event hasn't changed, but you process it differently.

The facts of the past generate different feelings at different times.

As a husband, I've had to calibrate what it means to show care for my wife, not just in light of previous facts but also in the context of present feelings. To my embarrassment, I've learned that I can convey a "calendar psychology" mindset: These historical events are in the past, so you need to move on. We're not talking about the past because it's already passed. I wonder if that's why some older couples have so little genuine conversation.

I've had to learn that knowing the particulars of what happened in the past isn't sufficient. My ongoing care for Bev needs to be characterized by a "Tell me more" spirit, where she doesn't just recount historical details but puts them in a current emotional frame. I need to retain an ongoing commitment to hearing her past story as she experiences it in the present. Even though I know the facts.

Pause and Reflect

If we want to know a person well, we show interest in their ongoing and ever-changing feelings about historical facts.

Free-Associating

ALTHOUGH I'VE HAD EXCELLENT EYESIGHT all my life, I was diagnosed with central retinal vein occlusion a few years ago. It comes about when the blood supply into the eye gets blocked. At the time of diagnosis, the specialist gave me a booklet that encouraged me to get counseling from the Canadian National Institute for the Blind to prepare for the potential of that outcome.

It was daunting to go from years of excellent vision to the prospect of limited or no vision.

Not long after the diagnosis, I ran into an old acquaintance I hadn't talked to for years. While catching each other up on our lives, I mentioned that I'd just been diagnosed with central retinal vein occlusion.

"Really?" he responded. "My neighbor just got that, and she's gone completely blind."

We all act this way at times. A word, a phrase, an incident gets our attention. We free-associate, tell our anecdote, and in the process, simply use someone else's story to tell our own. As was the case with my acquaintance, there are times when our response is quite uncaring. The last thing I needed to hear at that moment was that my fear of going blind might become a reality.

The amygdala is the part of the brain that responds instinctively and with emotion when presented with something that triggers a personal experience from our own lives. We've all been in social situations that cause our amygdala to trigger.

You begin talking about your upcoming trip to Japan, and the other person uses that to talk about their recent holiday. You then share a little about your parenting struggles, and that's met with "Tell me about it," and you're subjected to a lengthy monologue on their parenting. You leave the evening feeling like everything you shared was used as a springboard for the other person to do a deep dive into telling you their story.

I love spending time with people who wait, listen, and communicate, inviting me—both verbally and nonverbally—to tell them more. When you're around people like this, you have a sense of being cared for, understood, and heard. It's a gift that you welcome and that you want to give in return.

Pause and Reflect

If we believe in the sacredness and significance of other people's stories, we'll give them the gift of listening attentively to their experiences.

Compassion, Not Solutions

IT WAS ONE OF THOSE "meet over dinner for a preliminary conversation before the formal job interview" events.

One of the two men came to meet me in the lobby, and we exchanged pleasantries as we walked to the table. We were both a little awkward, overtalking with intensity. He introduced me to his colleague, and before any of us sat down, he asked, "Do you have a family?"

When Bev and I were diagnosed with infertility three years into our marriage, we were devastated. Everyone we knew was having babies, many of them on their "first try," a challenging phrase for those who tried many times. Our initial coping style was to stay quiet: The *I* word was too painful to link with our experience and too overwhelming to say aloud.

We then arrived at a place where we were able to admit it to others. We weren't alone. Others were also struggling. Saying *infertility* out loud was appropriate.

Before I sat in my chair, my response to the question was straightforward. "No. My wife and I struggle with infertility."

Before he sat in his chair, and just as the ". . . ity" was out of my mouth, he asked, "Have you ever tried vitamin E?"

What? You hardly know my name, have never met me, just found out I struggle with infertility, and now you have a solution? Vitamin E? What would I put it on? Or in? For how long?

Solution-oriented people are on the lookout for problems. Articulation of difficulties, troubles, and predicaments is an occasion for answers, explanations, and remedies. Not infrequently, articulating the problem doesn't need depth or detail for solution-oriented people to offer a remedy. Infertility is linked quickly with vitamin E.

In the absence of "Tell me more," my new friend doesn't know anything about our lived experience with infertility. "My wife and I struggle with infertility" is an objective statement, but what meaning do Bev and I bring to it? Maybe we've pursued every potential solution, including vitamin E, and are exhausted in the process. Perhaps the diagnosis is recent, and we're numb, unable to explore any ways forward.

Bringing instant solutions to others' problems may give us a sense of control and competence, but it minimizes care and compassion by keeping relationships at a superficial level.

Pause and Reflect

If we offer compassion when others have problems, we acknowledge their value and affirm their lived experience.

Labeling without Listening

AN ACQUAINTANCE OF MINE has a unique way of referencing his three children in conversation. If you're at a social event with him and ask, "Do you have any children?" he responds, "Yes; two Republicans and a Democrat." What? No names and ages? No gender or geographic location?

Once you get by the oddness of such a response, you realize he's not alone. Many of us depersonalize others by elevating categories and fitting people into them. "What else would you expect? He's an artist." "Of course, she's going to express herself that way. She's an engineer." "Everyone knows how professors think."

When we presume that everyone can be classified as a Republican or Democrat, artist, engineer, or professor and fit nicely into our preconceived boxes, it's an efficient way to function relationally. We don't need to hear any more about them; we have them all figured out.

If we're struggling with others, labeling also seems to serve us well. I worked in an organization where there was some disrespect and even disdain for the group that certified our product. One of the staff referred to that group as the "suits in _____," naming the city. I've also been involved in businesses where the board and administration referenced the staff by suggesting "inmates were running the asylum." No need to say "Tell me more" to the certification group or the staff. Label assigning leads to avoiding conflict resolution.

Families can also fall into the trap of labeling by overemphasizing particular attributes. When a mother references "my rebellious son" and a husband consistently describes his partner as "the wife," their labels are revealing.

A son is much more than his behavior, and a partner is much more than "the wife." They have names, are in relationships with other people, and have stories to share and lives to understand. Extending a "Tell me more" invitation will move them beyond a depersonalized label and into a more profound sense of who they are.

Pause and Reflect

If we relate to people only through the labels we assign them, we don't invite them to tell us more.

Overwhelmed by Experiences

I BECAME GOOD FRIENDS with a married man in his twenties through participating in the same community and sharing mutual interests. A few years into our relationship, he said he wanted to tell me his story in more detail, so we arranged a time and place. As we sat down, his body language and facial expressions told me that he'd drop a bomb. He did.

"I was born female. I had gender-reassignment surgery when I was younger."

We've all been through moments of this sort. One sentence is spoken, and we instantly feel overwhelmed. We're unsure what to say as we experience a racing heart and increasing anxiety, disbelief, and unexplainable fear.

What could I say to this person, who looks like a man and has always been a man to me? What are the options in this situation?

"Tell me more."

When we're exposed to other peoples' experiences, we can feel weighed down, thinking we have to say the right thing in the right way with the right outcome. But my friend wasn't looking for a solution. He didn't want an answer to a question. He was relaying his story, and all he needed was a "Tell me more" response.

In the presence of unexpected problems or experiences, most of us have so much self-absorbed anxiety about what we should do or say that we're paralyzed in our ability to care for others.

I tell some people I saw a psychiatrist for several years and have been on antidepressant medication for a long time. It's striking how many of them nod quietly but want the conversation to end. I know many individuals who have experienced or been close to those who have gone through psychiatric hospitalization, imprisonment, suicide attempts, death by suicide, death of a child, and the like. When they share about their reality, their lived experience is that others, be it acquaintances, friends, or family, would prefer the sound of silence.

All too frequently, you hear a seemingly appropriate line, like—"I didn't want to bring it up in case it upsets her / gets him thinking about it / will make it worse / will move her out of a positive place." It makes you wonder why other peoples' stories are so threatening to us.

Pause and Reflect

If we become overwhelmed with other peoples' experiences, we limit the opportunity for them to tell us their stories.

Personality Tests

I ONCE ATTENDED a conference on the role of personality in the workplace. We were handed a blank name tag and a felt pen at the registration table. It wasn't our name that was to appear on the sticker but our Myers-Briggs designation.

Based on four dichotomies of the Myers-Briggs Type Indicator—Introversion or Extraversion, Sensing or Intuition, Thinking or Feeling, Judging or Perceiving— we were to identify our four-letter acronym (like ESTJ or INTP) and stick it on our shirt.

Recently, the Enneagram, a similar but different device, has become popular. With the Enneagram, a number replaces four letters: Each number between one and nine is assigned a different personality type.

There's debate about whether such devices are grounded in sound science and a concern that they create a false sense of self and others. But cocktail parties often come to life when personality types are discussed.

The risk is that devices of this nature can minimize what it means to be human and lessen stories' centrality in our unique experiences of life. "I had to leave the job—I'm an *I*, and it was a people place." "My marriage is driving me crazy—he's a *T*, and I'm an *F*." "Obviously, I have trouble fitting in—I'm a Four." "You shouldn't be surprised that I'm angry all the time—I'm a One."

What are the stories behind being an introvert, having marital tension, not fitting in, or experiencing perpetual anger? We often lack the time and interest to provide space for others to share their story, so it's easy to stick with the letter, the single word, or the number. We assume we know everything there is to know.

Maybe someone has experienced immense fear and shame, and the apparent introversion is a way to cope. Marriage is a strange and complicated relationship with many dynamics that can't be fully captured in words like *thinking* or *feeling*. Not fitting in may be traced to many factors, including inappropriate ways of relating or unwelcoming communities. Anger may relate to historical pain or abandonment or might be an appropriate response to a traumatic event. Saying "Tell me more" is a lot more work than hearing a number or letter, but it's a wonderful relational investment.

Pause and Reflect

If we rely heavily on personality tests, we may not expend the time and energy to listen to people's stories.

Counseling Process

I'VE BEEN TO SEVEN different counselors in my life. On two occasions, it related to family-of-origin issues, two concentrated on parenting and marriage dynamics, two focused on my journey with depression, and one helped with a vocational transition.

Although the stigma on mental health and counseling has lessened, there are still odd stereotypes about the sector. For some people, going to seven counselors indicates I'm a sick puppy who's having trouble functioning. Those who view life through the grid of control and competence wonder why anyone would need that many helpers. Solver-fixer types interpret having seven counselors as a reflection that I'm not being given the right advice. People who struggle with vulnerability can't fathom journeying to that many counseling offices.

Even though the counselors came from different perspectives, and the problems I presented were diverse, one thing brought it all together: They all asked me to tell them more.

It isn't enough to say there are issues in my family of

origin, struggles in my marriage and parenting, angst in my journey with depression, or confusion in my vocational direction. Each of these categories is a window into my life. They aren't merely questions that require an answer, problems that require a solution, or experiences that need a fix. Together they make up who I am.

With wisdom and empathy, all my counselors helped me open up. When I wanted to tell the story briefly, even superficially, I was invited into a space where welcome and hospitality produced more detail. My sense of aloneness in pain led to an encounter of copilgrimage, where someone was walking with me. As my openness increased, the counselors engaged with encouragement, information, skill development, guidance, and perspective.

Counseling is an environment where you are being heard by the counselor and by yourself. When someone else says, "Tell me more," it provides them with an opportunity for a deeper understanding of you. Explaining your experiences to someone else can increase your own self-understanding in the process.

Pause and Reflect

If we engage in the counseling process, we open up not just to the counselor but also to ourselves.

Listening to Strangers

CONFESSION: I've had a lifelong addiction to dessert. Not carrot cake, zucchini bread, fruit, and the like but real dessert. Chocolate. Pastries. Cake. Cookies.

When the restaurant server comes over after the first course is finished and says, "Would you like dessert?" I usually say, "Is the pope Catholic?" The implication is clear.

Bev and I were sitting in a Florida restaurant, and the young server came to the table. She asked the usual question, and I asked mine. Her response was startling. "Is he?" To which I responded, "Tell me more."

We proceeded to have a twenty-minute conversation about her family history, her parents' adverse reaction to religion, and her confusion about the church and its role in society. She had no idea what it meant to be Catholic, who the pope was, and what role he played. There was intrigue and curiosity as she spoke, and while I found the move from dessert to religion jarring, it was clear that her move from server to conversation partner was welcomed and appreciated.

As I get older, I realize how my treatment of the stranger

keeps them in that place. If I never ask them to tell me more or allow them to tell their story, I don't provide an opportunity to express care.

That's been the case with my barber. (I did say "barber," not "hairstylist.") He's cut my hair for over twenty years, but it's all too easy to keep him in that functionary role. *I have hair. It needs to be cut. He's a barber. We have a match.*

Several years ago, we began sharing our experience as dads. We've both spent hours in the hospital with our children. He'd ask me about my experiences, and I'd tell him. I'd do the same in return, and I began realizing that he wasn't merely a barber but a *person.*

This reality came to the surface in a poignant way when one of his children died. It was painful to hear him recount the story and relay raw emotions. He was still cutting my hair, but he was no longer just a barber.

Pause and Reflect

If we invite the stranger to tell us more, we make a connection that may take us into unexplored territory.

Issues and Faces

WHATEVER MIGHT PROVOKE a dispute, heated discussion, controversy, or opposing viewpoints is now called an "issue." We have issues like social justice, poverty, prostitution, refugees, homelessness, LGBTQ+, and abortion. An issue focus leads to questions like "What's your position on this issue?" or "Where do you stand on this issue?"

No names. No faces. No stories. Just issues.

I used to drive by a houseless older woman as I turned into our townhouse parking lot. Poorly dressed and unkempt, she'd push a stolen shopping cart laden with everything imaginable. Some days you couldn't even see her over all the junk. I never got close enough to check, but she looked like she smelled. With all the middle-class humility I could muster, I often wondered why she lived this way.

When the issues of poverty and homelessness were debated in our city, I'd sometimes think about the woman with the cart, but rarely.

One day I had an overwhelming sense that I should talk to her. The lady now has a name.

I'm on a first-name basis with Lilly now. We talk about our lives regularly. I seldom go past her without stopping. I no longer put coins in the hats of poor people on the side of the street. We give money regularly—not to the poor but to Lilly.

She sleeps under a bridge about two hundred yards from where I sleep. When I queried that decision, she wondered why anyone would want to sleep in a hostel with alcoholics and drug addicts. She keeps up on the news by going on a computer at the local library and often tells me things that I didn't know.

When friends and family come to visit, we introduce them to Lilly. My sister and my daughter have given her Christmas presents, and last year, when we were thinking of who to ask over for Christmas, Lilly was on the list.

Issue is such an interesting word.

Our current interest in justice issues runs the risk of being conceptual, ideological, and political, even moralistic. No longer can I think of homelessness and poverty in that way. Lilly is a person. She has a name and a story. And when I hug her, the impact remains.

Pause and Reflect

If social justice concerns are framed as issues, we'll miss the reality that every issue has a face, a name, and a story.

Diagnoses with Curiosity

AS WE WALKED down the maternity ward, we could hear the baby's heartbeat. Our excitement was off the scale. I had my smelling salts ready for the delivery. What new father wants to pass out while the mother is going through so much pain and trauma?

On November 29, 1987, at 8:22 p.m., the teenager who wanted us to adopt her baby gave birth to Jessica Noel.

There was no noise. Her head, severely misshapen by the excessive suction, was the size of an eight-month-old baby and filled with cerebral spinal fluid. Before long, she was in an ambulance, then taken to a university hospital, where she underwent two neurosurgeries. She came home from the hospital with a diagnosis of idiopathic aqueductal stenosis.

Three years later, she grew a single breast and was diagnosed with precocious puberty, a rare condition, which in her case was caused by excessive brain pressure on the pituitary gland.

Over the subsequent ten years, two more diagnostic labels were added—frontal-lobe brain damage and high-functioning autism—and by the time she reached her early thirties, she'd been an inpatient or in a hospital-emergency department over fifty times.

Bev and I have valued people in our lives who've gone beyond the labels. They've journeyed with us, saying "Tell me more," both in spirit and in words. But what has surprised me most about myself and others is how easy it is not to adopt that posture with Jessica Noel herself.

When we focus on the label, a designation given by medical professionals, we treat the person like an object—someone to observe. From a depersonalized distance, it's easier not to connect. Not to be curious. Not to care.

But what's been eye-opening is hearing my daughter's own experience with her challenges. It's been much easier to care for Jessica by saying, "Tell me more" when I've moved past the objective diagnoses from professionals to her lived reality. Being curious about her experiences is much more valuable than knowing her diagnoses.

Pause and Reflect

If we look beyond diagnostic labels, we liberate others and ourselves to discover the uniqueness of their humanity.

Limited Privilege

I DON'T FEEL GUILTY for being a Caucasian male from the Republic of Ireland, but I'm aware that my skin color, gender, and ethnicity have brought privilege. People who look like me get hired with greater frequency, experience more promotions, and receive higher compensation. Doors were opened for me that weren't unbolted for people of color, for women, or for those of a different ethnic background.

Privilege has two first cousins: blindness and deafness. When you hold a perspective of privilege, you don't see and hear from those who lack privilege. Their stories are untold. Their experiences are muted. Their perspectives are obscured.

Early in President Franklin Roosevelt's tenure, affirmative action gained momentum around race, color, creed, and gender. Particular minorities were being discriminated against, and some people felt that this prejudice could be rectified by taking intentional steps toward including these minorities in the room.

Over the years, I've participated in communities that approached this topic negatively and positively.

In one community, a calculated decision led to welcoming women, people of color, and those from diverse ethnic backgrounds. I found it interesting to hear the viewpoint of people who weren't like me. As they relayed their stories and offered their opinions, the uniqueness of their contributions struck me. Their foundational arguments came from a different perspective, and their sociocultural template was refreshing. I found the environment stimulating as minority voices told me more.

In another community, there was an adverse reaction against affirmative action. Welcoming minorities was discriminating against the majority. While there were no firmly held negative attitudes toward women or people from other cultures, those groups weren't well represented. We debated the pros and cons of affirmative action, but we didn't hear from those who were left out, even as we engaged in the debates about them. I knew how white Western men approached the world, but I wanted to ask others to tell me more.

If they aren't in the room, it's hard to see and hear others.

Pause and Reflect

If we invite the nonprivileged into the room, we'll be less blind and deaf to others' stories.

Misunderstanding Actions

IT WAS A SPEAKING EVENT with about 150 people in attendance, most of whom I knew superficially and others more personally. About halfway through my talk, a gentleman stood up, moved down the aisle toward the door, and left.

If you've done public speaking of any sort, you know how the process unfolds. You continue to express yourself externally, but the brain chatter is intense. *Did I say something wrong? Is he upset? I thought he didn't like me. I wonder what point triggered him?*

As the week went on, I constructed an elaborate narrative in my head. I knew what he was thinking, which point triggered him, and why he walked out in frustration. It's stunning how easy it is to put the fragments together. We have no idea what was going on in moments like these, but our objective assessment and detailed clarity about them are remarkable.

I've learned that the best way to determine whether my sophisticated internal stories are accurate is to say, "Tell me more" to the other person. So, I made the phone call.

"Jeremy. It's Rod." And before I had a chance to say anything else, he says, "I'm so sorry I left your talk the other night. I was enjoying it, but I had to pee. I didn't come back in because I didn't want to disrupt you."

It's easy to observe other peoples' behavior, blend in our own dynamics, sprinkle in judgment, and create egocentric conclusions. When we're missing the story that lurks behind the action, we have no idea what's going on, but we fool ourselves into believing we're dead right.

In my own life, two important stories have shaped who I am regarding the topic of family. One occurred when I was in utero and the other when I was five. If you observed my family-of-origin relationships and my marriage and parenting dynamics, you'd accurately find that these have been areas of episodic strain. I have no sense that those two early narratives victimized me, and I take full responsibility for my behavior. But without a "Tell me more," you wouldn't know my complete perspective on family.

Pause and Reflect

If we strive to understand other people's stories, we lessen the risk of misunderstanding their actions.

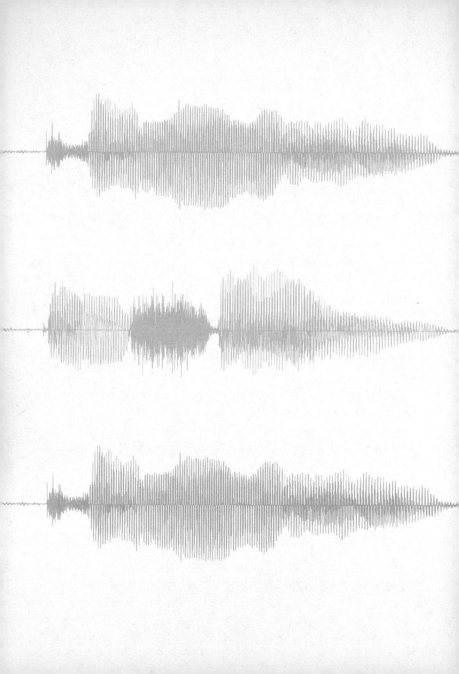

Part Four

Imagine a World

IMAGINE A WORLD WHERE SAYING "Thank you" were noticeable. A world where we acknowledged the positive impact others have on us. Gratitude would increase as entitlement decreased.

Imagine a world where saying "I'm sorry" were conspicuous. A world where we acknowledged the negative impact we have on others. Remorse would increase as victimization decreased.

Imagine a world where "Tell me more" were evident. A world where we acknowledged the impact we have on each other. Care would increase as individualism decreased.

Imagine what it would be like to journey together on a planet where we affirmed our kinship. Our inherent connectedness with one another would be a cause for celebration, as we saw all others as fellow offspring deserving of our gratitude, remorse, and care.

We'd add more faith as the world embraced cynicism. We'd supply more hope as the world experienced despair. We'd contribute more love, as the world faced hate.

If saying "Thank you"," I'm sorry," and "Tell me more" brought the world more faith, hope, and love, that would be enough.

I want that for the world, your world, and my world.

Epilogue

Being Christian

IF YOU'VE REACHED this part of the book, you may have had enough. You read about gratitude, remorse, and care, and you hope to practice what you learned. Knowing my *why* for writing the book and coming to grips with what it means to be Christian aren't particularly interesting to you. If this is you, I bid you farewell.

When I was a kid, I remember learning the biblical Creation story and being struck by God's obsession with the word *good*.[1] He created light, and it was good. Land and sea? It was good too. Couldn't we call the creation of vegetation, plants, and trees *beautiful*? No. They were good as well. Then the sun and the moon were scrutinized. Good. The creation of animals? That, too, was good. And when humanity arrived and Creation was complete, God looked at it all and said that it was "very good."[2]

One option to explain this is that God had a limited vocabulary, so he had no other choice but to repeat the word *good*. But that would be to miss the biblical word's immensity. Reflecting something desirable and delightful, *good* speaks to flourishing and expansiveness, wholeness and harmony. As Creation unfolded, the pieces began to fit together, and the overall beauty of it all blossomed.

But then, out of the blue, comes a strange declaration from God. "It is not good." Such a jarring phrase to drop into the account of Creation. After the excessive repetition of the word *good*, now something God created is not good? A good creation is now designated as imperfect. Less than ideal.

When you push into the narrative's details, you realize that the "not good" description is even more shocking. Adam, the created man, is in a beautiful garden with unique surroundings, delighting in it all. Pain, anguish, sin, and brokenness haven't entered the scene yet. And, more importantly, Adam is in an unflawed relationship with God. What could be better?

It would be a massive oversight to miss the importance of this moment in the story. A human being living on an unspoiled planet has no tension in his relationship with the Creator. It is a picture-perfect environment that seems like the ultimate lived experience. But even God himself designates the situation as "not good." How interesting that a perfect relationship with God may not be enough, or at least not good.

The phrase following "It is not good" is simple and straightforward. "It is not good that the man should be alone; I will make him a helper as his partner."[3] Although marriage and family concerns often get linked with this statement, it also has profound things to say about what it means to be human. It's an early description of the way we are. We aren't solitary, autonomous individuals in an idyllic relationship with God. Instead, we relate to the other. Our connection isn't just to God but to all things he has created.

Adam learned that he didn't exist in isolation. And his relationship with God wasn't his only sense of connection. Upon receiving Eve through God's creative action, he now had the opportunity to understand intimacy with another. I wonder if it puzzled him that another created being, not God, would be his suitable helper? He had trust, solidarity, and well-being with the Creator, but now he was invited to experience these things with Eve too.

God revealed something significant in the Creation account. His passion for humanity isn't confined to relationship with him and with all the nonhuman things he created. How we relate to others is just as important. That is why it shouldn't be a surprise to see him delivering the Ten Commandments.[4]

In contemporary culture, the term *commandment* seems archaic and out of touch, an imposition of power that needs truth spoken into it. Or maybe the expression of a narcissistic god who outlines arbitrary demands that are only for religious zealots. The commandments have a sacred ring about them that doesn't fit the secularity of this point in time.

But when you look at the list of ten in detail, it becomes evident that, like the Creation account, they're focused on our lives' vertical and horizontal trajectories. The first three stress the importance of no other gods, no false images, and no misuse of God's name, respectively. The fourth places value on taking a day per week to follow the Creator's example and not work, so you, others, and your animals all experience rest. The following six focus on the importance of honoring parents and avoiding murder, adultery, stealing, lying, and coveting, respectively.

In total, the Ten Commandments bring significance to reverencing God and respecting others. They value contentment over coveting, truth over lying, work over stealing, commitment over adultery, life over murder, and honor over disrespect. They accord the Creator God his rightful place and invite all of us to have a healthy relationship to work. That doesn't seem too hyperspiritual to me.

And did you notice the numerical breakdown of the commandments? Three focus on our relationship with the Creator, one emphasizes the need for us to use the Creator as our example for work rhythms, and six are about how we relate to others. God seems to know where our main struggles reside.

If you read through the rest of the Hebrew Scriptures, you'll find plentiful evidence that humanity doesn't just have problems with God but also with each other. And not infrequently, those who seem to be closest to God are the most disrespectful of others. Alignment with the Creator doesn't always guarantee appreciation for his human creation.

When the angelic hosts announced the birth of Jesus, it was a twofold message: "Glory to God in the highest heaven, and on earth peace."[5] Messiah's arrival was an opportunity for people to look vertically and be thankful to God for the gift of his Son. But it was also an invitation to bring a horizontal perspective. Jesus brought the goodwill and peace we need to infuse in our relationships with one another. Being a follower of Jesus had profound implications for both the highest heaven and the earth.

Having a faith that is expressed in our human interactions can be an insult to the über-religious. They highly value their relationship with God as they define him and see the development of that relationship as the height of spirituality, the ultimate in holiness. If they were asked to cast a ballot, they would vote for God being the priority and people being a distant second. One is more sacred and transcendent, the other much more secular and material. They might agree with the saying, "I love God; it's people that drive me crazy."

I suspect this kind of thinking led the New Testament's Pharisees to ask Jesus which commandment was the greatest. His answer, as always, was profound. "You want to know what all the law and the prophetic writings hang on [he did say 'hang'!]? *Love God. Love your neighbor.*"[6] In these two simple statements, Jesus summarized the first part of the Ten Commandments and the second; love God and love others.

But that answer wasn't enough for the religious leaders. They wanted Jesus to define *neighbor*, so he told the story of the Good Samaritan. A man is robbed, beaten, and left for dead. Respectable individuals like a priest and a Levite pass him by, but a Samaritan man stops, shows love, and brings healing. A Samaritan, linked with a despised cultural group that was perceived as an enemy by the Jews. When Jesus ended the story, he asked the question that had started the conversation. "Who was the neighbor?" The Pharisees couldn't avoid the answer. "The one who gave mercy."[7] Love has no cultural boundaries.

When the apostle Paul picks up this theme in his writings, he talks about loving one another as a continuing debt and doing no harm to neighbors.[8] We never come to the place where we can say "My love for others is complete." We always have a responsibility to act in a way that helps the other. The capacity to harm people is still present, but the invitation is an ongoing commitment to love. Throughout all the New Testament letters, there are constant reminders that our faith shows its colors in our relationships with each other.

Many of us have acquired definitions of love through popular music and an oversexualized culture. In those two arenas, love makes us feel good, gives us energy, aids our self-esteem, and makes our world go round. When you experience that kind of love, you're ecstatic and emotional, overcome by inner sensations, sexual and otherwise, making you feel great. But therein lies the problem: you.

Biblical love is sacrificial, hard work, others-oriented. Engaging in this kind of love might not make you feel good at all. Think of parenting. Loving children is sometimes one of the most painful forms of love one can experience. Frequently neither the parents nor the child is happy, but doing what is best for the other isn't always easy. An attentiveness to the other, an inclination in their direction, is a move away from ourselves. That is why the phrase "falling in love" is such a contradiction. Falling requires no energy or effort. But real love requires all of that and more.

For Christians, a life of love is built on the fact that we are loved.[9] Vertical understanding that God loves me opens up my horizontal world, where all others are recipients of my love. All others. Those who are easy to love, and those who are challenging to love. Even enemies. Even Samaritans. Even those who disagree. Even Republicans. Even Democrats.

Our capacity to love the other reflects our understanding of God's love for us. A seeming inability or apparent unwillingness to love others may reflect a lack of appreciation for his love. Being good with God and not with others isn't Christian.[10]

Gratitude, remorse, and care are three ways we can acknowledge the other. When we express gratitude to others, communicating that they have influenced us positively, we value them. When we show remorse to others, conveying that we have affected them negatively, we cherish them. When we communicate care to others, letting them know we want to hear their story, we respect their dignity. In doing so, we are loving people.

But despite what our leader said, we aren't always known by our love.[11]

There were many positive influences from the church where I grew up, but one of their significant contributions hasn't served me well: *us* and *them*. This was a long time ago, and is by no means typical of most contemporary churches, but many of us have had to wrestle through this particular issue.

This simple distinction expressed itself in various ways. Communion was only for certain people, and they would sit in a circle around a table with bread and wine. Just outside the circle were two sets of chairs. The males sat on one side, while the females sat on the other. All the children and several adults were in those outside locations, meaning that children didn't sit with their parents, and some spouses and singles weren't part of the circle on Sunday morning. These two sets of chairs were described in various ways: "Seat of the unlearned." "Goat pen." "Back seat."

The economy of that church on a Sunday morning was transparent. Those in the circle were *us*. Those outside the circle were *them*.

I remember with pain the not-infrequent experiences of having one of the leaders invite all those in the back seats to go outside. We would get up without our parents, go down the stairs and out to the church's front lawn. About ten minutes later, people would come out in tears, with sad faces, because someone had been "read out." The following week we'd find out who the person was because they'd be seated in the goat pen with the rest of us. Excommunication in our church meant you moved from *us* to *them* because of a particular sin. Moving out of the circle into a "seat of the unlearned" was a loud message.

At youth events, we were warned that we shouldn't become too friendly with two groups of people—non-Christians and Christians outside our particular church brand. High school was such a weird experience for me because only one fellow student was linked with our churches. The *us* comprised two people, and the other twelve hundred students were the *them*—those who were not following Jesus at all or who were not following him in the right way. My only way to survive was to disobey church rules and have "too many" friends.

When my wife and I left that church and moved from an *us* to a *them* position, it was made very clear that we were moving out from under God's protection and that any pain we experienced could be traced to this less-than-honorable decision. Several months after my parents left the same church and my father had a heart attack, my mother received a community leader's visit. As she was sitting on a chair outside her husband's hospital room, experiencing anguish over his physical well-being, she was told that now she knew which church she should be attending. Leaving *us* and becoming *them* had significant medical consequences.

It would be easy to dismiss these events as strange experiences from a time long ago, but *us* and *them* is still alive and well.

Within and between churches and Christian nonprofits, individuals and groups continue to allocate members of our tribe into one box or the other. Relational fractures are extensive as we head to our *us* and *them* corners. Conservatives demonize liberals based on their beliefs and offer them a seat in the goat pen. Liberals who find conservatives' behavior out of touch with contemporary thinking point them to their place in the seat of the unlearned.

Those outside the church observe us as we discuss and debate sexism and racism, homophobia and social justice, immigration and globalization, and they sense the thread of fear and anger that pulls a lot of it together. They react not just to the content of our beliefs but to our attitudes toward others. When they feel like *them*, as we elevate *us*, we don't endear ourselves to them, and they aren't interested in what we have to offer. It's hard to comprehend what's going on in the circle when you're on the outside looking in.

Where will we find hope?

As diverse perspectives on beliefs and behaviors create distance within the Christian community and between that community and all others, we need to grasp the importance of belonging.

We are connected to one another. Rooted in the way we were created and emphasized throughout biblical material, it's the way things are. Our responsibility is to express that link by loving the other. No limitations. No escape clauses because of beliefs. No avoidance because of behavior. All are acknowledged, respected, loved. We belong to each other.

When we express "Thank you," "I'm sorry," and "Tell me more" to the other, we strengthen our sense of belonging. We don't just affirm our understanding of God but also acknowledge the dignity of those he has created. We are all his offspring.[12]

The Human Library, housed in Denmark, is a facility where readers can borrow human beings to serve as open books. Suppose you want to find out about a group that has been subjected to prejudice or discrimination because of their social status, ethnic origin, disability, belief, lifestyle, or diagnosis. In that case, this library will provide human interaction to facilitate your learning. Not simply cognitive learning but a personal education.[13]

Library texts have their place, but there's something unique about being impacted by another person. Christianity is no different. If all we have to offer are concepts and ideas written on the page, even in our sacred text we call the Bible, we miss our faith's relational nature. Gratitude, remorse, and care are not disembodied concepts written on the pages of this book. They're much more than that.

Am I a Christian? Ask the people who interact with me.

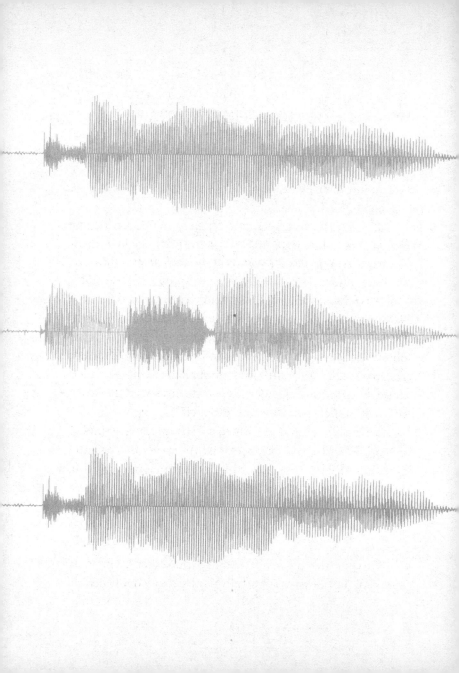

Acknowledgments

While I take full responsibility for everything contained herein, this book reflects many people's attentive diligence.

I am grateful for Peter Bachman, Andrew Chong, John Colpitts, Shaun Huberts, Isa Purcell, Sara Watkins, Ali Wilson, Mike Wilson, and Jessica Noel Wilson. As I was writing, they provided me with instructive feedback. Their observations led me to make various turns on the journey, and their charitable criticisms produced several discarded drafts. Their names are not on the front cover, but they contributed immensely to the end product.

I have been impressed with NavPress's ability to combine the professional with the personal. As they seek to create a quality project, they blend in a commitment to treating people with respect and dignity. It has been a joy to write a book on relationships produced by a staff that exemplifies those values. In particular, I would like to highlight three people.

Early in the process, NavPress publisher Don Pape engaged the ideas thoughtfully and provided invaluable feedback that helped shape the book's structure. I appreciate his engagement, humor, and advocacy.

Copy editors are invaluable but frightening to those of us who write. Elizabeth Schroll is a superb copy editor. She reads carefully and fairly and critiques with grace and humor. I am grateful for her role in this process.

David Zimmerman oversaw this project from beginning to end. His ability to bring a big-picture perspective, combined with his attention to detail and warm relationality, made for an enjoyable editorial partnership. I am thankful for how he stewards his considerable gifts and abilities.

Endorsing a book is a labor of love, a sacrifice of energy, and a leap of faith. I am deeply indebted to Dan Allender, Michael Blair, Michele Bland, Alia Eyres, Bob Inglis, Archbishop Michael Miller, Luci Shaw, Jamie Smith, Patti Towler, William Wan, and Keren Dibbens-Wyatt, who were willing to advocate publicly for this project from their various countries and sectors.

Finally, I want to thank my wife, Bev. My life and this book have been helped immeasurably by her commitment to reality and dislike of impression management. She read every word I wrote, brought encouragement and criticism as appropriate, and cheered me on when the journey was challenging. More than any other person, she has helped me understand the significance of "Thank you," "I'm sorry," and "Tell me more."

Discussion Guide

THE BEST WAY to absorb a book focused on relationships is to read and discuss it with others. Why not join together with a group of friends, colleagues, or family members, read the book, and then come together to tell stories, pursue wisdom, and encourage each other toward the pursuit of gratitude, remorse, and care? The following questions, which could be discussed in one session or over the course of three sessions, will kick-start that journey. Maybe your world will change.

Thank You

1. Reflect on your family, friendships, neighborhood, place of worship, and workplace, along with government, politics, and the culture in general. Where do you run across an attitude of entitlement ("I deserve it")?

2. As you observe all these spheres, where do you observe an attitude of gratitude ("Thank you")?

3. How do you respond to the proposal in the book that one of the ways we can combat entitlement is to engage in more gratitude?

4. Are there particular areas of your life where saying thank you is a real challenge? How has the book helped you do that more effectively?

5. As you read through these twenty vignettes, are there one or two of them that speak specifically to your lived experience on gratitude? In what way?

6. The book proposes that we have a "why" that becomes the foundation for saying thank you to others. What is your why for gratitude?

I'm Sorry

1. Reflect on your family, friendships, neighborhood, place of worship, and workplace, along with government, politics, and the culture in general. Where do you hear an attitude of victimization ("It's not my fault")?

2. As you observe all these spheres, where do you hear an attitude of remorse ("I'm sorry")?

3. How do you respond to the proposal in the book that one of the ways we can combat victimization is to practice remorse?

4. Are there particular areas of your life where saying I'm sorry is a real challenge? How has the book helped you do that more effectively?

5. As you read through these twenty vignettes, are there one or two of them that speak specifically to your lived experience with remorse? In what way?

6. The book proposes that we have a "why" that becomes the foundation for saying I'm sorry to others. What is your why for remorse?

Tell Me More

1. Reflect on your family, friendships, neighborhood, place of worship, and workplace, along with government, politics, and the culture in general. Where do you encounter an attitude of individualism ("My story matters most")?

2. As you observe all these spheres, where do you encounter an attitude of care ("Tell me more")?

3. How do you respond to the proposal in the book that one of the ways we can combat individualism is to engage in more care?

4. Are there particular areas of your life where saying "Tell me more" is a real challenge? How has the book helped you do that more effectively?

5. As you read through these twenty vignettes, are there one or two of them that speak specifically to your lived experience with care? In what way?

6. The book proposes that we have a "why" that becomes the foundation for saying tell me more to others. What is your why for care?

Notes

INTRODUCTION: CHANGE THE WORLD?

1. Friedrich Nietzsche, "Maxims and Interludes," in *Beyond Good and Evil: Prelude to a Philosophy of the Future,* trans. R. J. Hollingdale (New York: Penguin Classics, 1990), 107.
2. This information on cargo ships and tugboats comes from my friend Ian Wright, who works in the industry.
3. The remaining 6 percent of religions are associated with particular ethnic or tribal groups. Data from "World Population by Religion," https://www.worldometers.info/world-population/#religions. Based on 2010 world population data.

THANK YOU

1. M. Tullius Cicero, *The Orations of Marcus Tullius Cicero,* trans. C. D. Yonge (London: George Bell & Sons, 1891), chap. 33, sec. 80.
2. On the benefits of gratitude, see "31 Benefits of Gratitude: The Ultimate Science-Backed Guide," https://www.happierhuman.com/benefits-of-gratitude/ and Amy Morin, "7 Scientifically Proven Benefits of Gratitude That Will Motivate You to Give Thanks Year-Round," *Forbes,* November 23, 2014, https://www.forbes.com/sites/amymorin/2014/11/23/7-scientifically-proven-benefits-of-gratitude-that-will-motivate-you-to-give-thanks-year-round/?sh=4fef48fe183c.

WHINY SPACE

1. See Steven Parton, "The Science of Happiness: Why Complaining Is Literally Killing You," March 14, 2018, https://medium.com/@ stevenparton/the-science-of-happiness-why-complaining-is-literally -killing-you-8aae6c5a4008.

ALL ABOUT ME

1. For more on narcissistic personality disorder, here's a good general reference: Cynthia Lechan Goodman and Barbara Leff, *The Everything Guide to Narcissistic Personality Disorder* (Avon, MA: Adams Media, 2011).

I'M SORRY

1. Emily Dickinson, "Remorse is Memory Awake," in *The Complete Poems of Emily Dickinson* (Boston: Backbay Books, 1961), 744.

ACT OF LISTENING

1. These and other indigenous peoples are native to their particular area, predating those who arrived later.

TELL ME MORE

1. Madeleine L'Engle, *Sold into Egypt: Joseph's Journeys into Human Being* (Wheaton, IL: Shaw, 1989), 15. Joseph's story is told in the Hebrew Bible, Genesis 37–50.
2. For example, see John 4:1-42.
3. For example, see John 3:1-21.
4. For example, see Mark 10:17-31.

FACTS AND FEELINGS

1. Genesis 3:7.

EPILOGUE: BEING CHRISTIAN

1. Genesis 1:4, 10, 12, 18, 21, 25.
2. Genesis 1:31.

3. Genesis 2:18, NRSV.

4. Exodus 20:1–17.

5. Luke 2:14, NRSV.

6. Matthew 22:36-40, author's paraphrase.

7. Luke 10:25-37.

8. Romans 13:8-10.

9. 1 John 4:19.

10. 1 John 4:8.

11. John 13:35.

12. Acts 17:29.

13. See https://humanlibrary.org/.

A Note on the Cover Design

THE PREMISE OF THIS BOOK is so simple: If we make it our practice to more often demonstrate gratitude, repentance, and curiosity in our relationships—where we live, work, play, study, and pray—we will become people who are more settled in our souls, more winsome in our witness. In doing so we model for the people around us a lifestyle that is gracious, grace-giving, humble, and relational. And in that modeling we inspire and empower others to do the same. These are world-changing habits.

This is, indeed, a book on habits. While it is grounded in theology, philosophy, and psychology, it is not a matter merely for intellectual curiosity. It's not merely interesting that saying "Thank you," "I'm sorry," and "Tell me more" on a regular basis has the impact that it does. It's transformational. And transformation is an embodied experience.

The cover design for *Thank You. I'm Sorry. Tell Me More.* is meant to demonstrate this important distinction for the book. The graphics behind the text of the cover are the sonic patterns made when we speak these words. The pattern behind the phrase is what the phrase sounds like. They are sacred sounds because they have such transformational quality, because they reflect the character of God.

We hope you enjoy this book, a distillation of Rod Wilson's best thinking over the course of his illustrious career. But more than that, we hope you put it into practice: We hope you finish this book and start saying "Thank you" more consistently, saying "I'm sorry" when repentance is called for, saying "Tell me more" when there's more beneath the surface of what has been said. We hope this book transforms your world—and that through you, the world is changed for the better.